England

$10.00

S0-ADY-109

York

Laxton (Lexington)   Lincoln

Boston

King's Lynn

Springfield

Needham Market

Haverhill   Wrentham

Bedford   Cambridge   Toppesfield   Framlingham

Woburn   Ipswich

Braintree   Sudbury   Dedham

St. Albans   Groton

Oxford   Maldon

Chelmsford

Waltham Abbey   Billericay

Sandwich

Winchester

Brighton

A Legacy of Names

English Towns with American Counterparts

Elaine Borish

Illustrations by Sheila Acton

Blackmore Press, Shaftesbury, Dorset

First published by The Blackmore Press 1980.

© Elaine Borish 1980

ISBN 0 950 20752 7

Typeset and Printed in Great Britain by T. H. Brickell & Son Ltd.,
Longmead, Shaftesbury, Dorset and Bound by Pitman Press, Bath.

Contents

Preface

What's in the name of a town, the poet might have asked. A great deal—is the answer I might offer. This book is for anyone whose curiosity or imagination is caught by the sources and associations of similar place names.

Many American cities and towns were named for the places in England from which the first settlers emigrated. Early citizens took these names with them to the new world and thereby established a permanent bond with the native town left behind. Americans still feel the alliance deeply.

That Americans are intrigued with the familiar place names in Old England can be witnessed by the steady streams of modern pilgrims who visit such places as Plymouth or Boston—in England. While I regret that the number of visitors to other enjoyable towns with such evocative names as Framlingham or Dedham or Worcester are not so great, perhaps this book will increase those numbers. But even the arm-chair traveler can enjoy reading about the linking of one place with another. How did the name come to be chosen? What is the English town like now?

This is not a definitive study. Nor is it possible to list with certainty *all* of the connections that exist. The selections contained in this book, merely representative, give the meaningful associations of the English counterpart and a feeling of what that town is like today.

Barnstaple

Never mind the tasteless traffic patterns and tall buildings that characterize modern Barnstaple. Never mind the shops, department stores, and office buildings that line the High Street. Or the bus station built in the once bustling quay. It is still possible to visualize the active harbor scene of an earlier era and to become immersed in the economic activity and wealth that once characterized the old town.

With over a thousand years of history, Barnstaple, the North Devon town on the River Taw, is one of the oldest towns in Britain. In 930, it was an established Saxon borough known as Beardestaple, the Staple—Boundary or Market—of Bearda. It prospered over the centuries as an important market town and seaport, particularly for the expanding wool and cloth making industry. As such, the quay was an especially busy place and the center of Barnstaple life. Today, Barnstaple has taken on the predictable characteristics of ordinary, busy city life.

Evidence of the rich past is present everywhere. Spacious and elegant houses can be seen in the area around Trafalgar Lawn. High Street too has a number of later but interesting buildings including the Guildhall, built in 1826 in classical style. The School of Art at 42 High Street is a house of the early nineteenth century. For contrast, the Three Tuns Tavern goes back to the fifteenth century. The Westminster Bank, which was the House of Spanish Merchants much earlier in its career, has outstandingly fine plaster ceilings. And on Tuesdays and Fridays the Pannier Market is worth a visit. The vast covered area, filled with stalls purveying a variety of goods, recalls the centuries-old Barnstaple tradition of "going to market." Just opposite it is Butcher's Row, an arcade of open-fronted butchers' shops built in mid-nineteenth century but retaining the medieval practice of grouping shops of one kind together.

The thirteenth-century Church of St. Peter's, in the center of town, contains some interesting monuments which attest to the wealth of the seventeenth-century mercantile families. Elizabeth Delbridge is shown as she died in 1628 with her swaddled infant "of which she died in childbirth." Another monument on the wall between south aisle and chapel depicts a man comfortably in bed with his wife and child.

Next to the church is the fourteenth-century Chapel of St. Anne, now functioning as a small, local museum. When chapels were suppressed by Henry VIII in 1547, it became the town's grammar school for nearly four hundred years. Here John Gay received his education.

Born in Barnstaple in 1685, John Gay is known primarily as the author of *The Beggar's Opera*. Barnstaple is justly proud of its local literary celebrity and announces its claim, even in such mundane ways as the "John Gay Coffee Shop."

The appropriately-named Long Bridge of sixteen arches spans the River Taw and the ages. Dating from the thirteenth century, and rebuilt around 1437, it has been widened and improved and altered on a number of occasions through the centuries, but it manages to maintain much of its medieval work as well as its picturesque qualities.

The Long Bridge

The river bank between Long Bridge and Queen Anne's Walk constituted the old and lively town center. The pleasant colonnade known as Queen Anne's Walk dominates the area now. In front of this colonnade was the quay from which "six ships from North Devon joined Sir Francis Drake's fleet at Plymouth, and helped to defeat the Spanish Armada," proclaims a plaque on the wall. The graceful walk, built in 1609, was restored in 1714 and a statue added. Under Queen Anne's Statue is the Tome Stone. Again, a plaque explains its use. Elizabethan merchants sealed bargains by placing payment on the mushroom-shaped stone before witnesses.

2

Queen Anne's Walk

The dignity and elegance which characterized Barnstaple when the Chichesters dominated this part of Devon still exist in Arlington Court. This National Trust site (seven miles northeast of the town) is notable for its collections of shells, model ships, pewter, and carriages. It is the ancestral home of the Chichester family and of Sir Francis Chichester, famous navigator knighted for his epic voyage around the world in 1966.

But perhaps the event of most interest to Americans is a particular seventeenth-century event, the founding of Barnstable, Massachusetts. The General Court established, in 1639, three Cape Cod Settlements, replacing their original Indian names with those of English ports: Barnstable, Sandwich, Yarmouth. At the time when Barnstable was being settled, Barnstaple was enjoying the great prosperity which can still be seen in its elegant old houses.

The twin cities, Barnstable and Barnstaple, share not only the same names, but also similar appearances and functions. Both are set in harbors that look remarkably alike. Both are gateways—to Cape Cod and to North Devon—and centers for summer holiday trade. When Barnstable celebrated in 1939 the tercentenary of its founding, it received a replica of one of the treasures of Barnstaple, a silver gilt Steeple Cup made in 1589 during the reign of Queen Elizabeth I. The exquisite cup was given by old Barnstaple to the American counterpart. All of this may well conjure up in America thoughts of that other Town of a Thousand Years.

3

Bedford

Fifty miles north of London is the easy-to-reach county town of Bedford. Bedfordshire is a small county which even the guide books admit lacks the rich scenery which characterizes so much of England; "the least picturesque of the English counties," says the Blue Guide to England. Perhaps Bedford is spoiled by the approach to it. Factories and beds of brick-laying clay, the basis of a large brick industry, mar and scar the landscape. With such bad press notices and with such an unappealing preview, one may wonder, why bother to reach it at all?

Because Bedford is nevertheless a pleasant town on the pretty, meandering River Ouse, with an interesting, colorful, and ancient background. Pepys recorded his visit to the town in 1667 and called it "a good country town." It still is.

Bedford has made good use of its tree-lined river, and the locals are justifiably proud of the Embankment with its riverside walks and gardens on both sides and seats which provide restful oases.

Bedford Bridge

The five-arched bridge over the Ouse enhances the total picture. Turner painted Bedford Bridge, as have many others. The good-looking scene takes in the Swan Hotel, built for the Duke of Bedford in 1794. Further along the Embankment, just beyond the Swan, is the Bedford Museum with its specimens of local history. Nearby, the Cecil Higgins Art Gallery has a surprising collection which includes works by Turner and Dürer, bronzes by Epstein and Henry Moore. Plenty to do and see in Bedford without even leaving the river area!

A river crossing undoubtedly existed from the earliest times. The ancient town of Bedford was inhabited by Celtic and Roman settlers before being occupied by the Saxons in the seventh and eighth centuries. The river remained fordable here, and the Danes made frequent incursions on Bedford. They devastated the town in several raids, and the destruction by fire in 1010 is still in evidence on the tower of St. Peter's Church which bears the marks of that fire. Shortly after the Norman Conquest, a castle with a commanding view of the river was built, of which only the mound remains. Old Bedford Bridge, which superseded a timber bridge, was built in 1224 from stones of the demolished castle. The present bridge dates from 1813.

But the event in history which dominates the Bedford of today centers on John Bunyan. Bunyan was born at Harrowden, just south of Bedford. The son of a tinker, he himself became a tinker and thinker who developed deep religious convictions. In the village of Elstow, he spent his childhood, and there he remained after marriage until he moved a mile away, to Bedford, in 1655.

Elstow, worth the journey in itself, is known for its thirteenth-century abbey church, thirteenth-century cottages, and picturesque sixteenth-century Moot Hall. The Moot Hall contained in its ground floor six small shops to be used at fair times, while upstairs was the village meeting hall. Now the remarkable building houses a museum of seventeenth-century life associated with the time of John Bunyan.

John Bunyan began preaching in 1656 and continued to do so even after nonconformist preaching was made illegal. A plaque at the corner of Silver Street in Bedford indicates the site of the County Gaol where he was imprisioned from 1660 to 1672 for religious dissent. Another plaque on the bridge sites the Town Gaol where he spent a further brief period of imprisonment in 1677 and where he probably began work on his best seller, *The Pilgrim's Progress*.

Elstow Moot Hall

Remembrances of the man are everywhere. The Bunyan Meeting House in Mill Street is a memorial to him, and the Bunyan Museum adjoins this church. The Meeting House was rebuilt in 1850 on the site of the earlier meeting-place that he became pastor of upon release from prison in 1672. Its bronze doors, which recall the Baptistry doors in Florence, illustrate in bas-relief ten scenes from *The Pilgrim's Progress*. Bunyan's chair and the pulpit from which he preached are here, as is the door of his cell in the County Gaol.

Since Bedford achieved a claim to fame by imprisoning John Bunyan, it seems a form of justice that another Bedford worthy is John Howard (1726-90), the great prison reformer. His statue, sculptured by Sir Alfred Gilbert in 1894, the creator also of Eros in London's Piccadilly Circus, stands in St. Paul's Square.

Here in the town center of St. Paul's Square, just over the bridge and around the bustling market square, are Shire Hall, Town Hall, Corn Exchange, and—of course—St. Paul's Church.

St. Paul's is the major church of Bedford. With its embattled clerestory and aisles, it makes a handsome background for the statue. In the south chapel of the church is a brass to Sir William Harpur, who died in 1573, and his wife. Harpur amassed a fortune in London, became Lord Mayor in 1561, and left a bequest for the establishment of almshouses and other

6

charities. The Harpur Trust now supports four schools in Bedford. The facade of the Bedford Modern School in Harpur Street, built in 1833, has been retained for a large and handsome, newly-developed shopping complex.

In contrast to the over-restored St. Paul's, the church of St. Peter De Merton has Anglo-Saxon traces and a Norman central tower. On St. Peter's Green is the dominating motif of Bedford, a statue—as you might have guessed—of John Bunyan.

Bunyan lived in a time of religious persecution when many dissenters left from Bedford as well as from surrounding villages. One Peter Bulkeley, Puritan rector of Odell, ten miles northwest of Bedford, emigrated to Massachusetts in 1635. From Cambridge, he led a party of planters through the woods to found a new colony which was named "Concord."

That the New World beckoned Bedforshire people would seem to be indicated by the fact that Bedford appears as the name of a number of American cities—in New Jersey, Pennsylvania, Kentucky, Iowa, Indiana, Montana, Illinois, as well as Massachusetts.

Billericay

A visitor to Billericay, that old-world Essex town just twenty-five miles northeast of London, need not search very long for a feeling of involvement in American history, for in 1620 a group of residents left their homes on Billericay's High Street to board the Mayflower for the New World.

It was Christopher Martin of Billericay, one of a contingent of four or five of the city's natives, who financed the Mayflower adventure and provisioned the ship. The group included Martin's wife, the widow Marie Prower whom he had married in 1607; his stepson Solomon Prower; John Langerman, a bondservant who worked for a fixed period of time in exchange for payment of expenses; and possibly a Peter Browne.

Christopher Martin's signature was ninth on the list of elders witnessing the Mayflower Compact written before the ship landed to found a Christian settlement in the wilderness. Alas, many pilgrims succumbed during that first dreadful winter. William Bradford recorded of him: "He and all his, dyed in the first infection not long after the arrival" including an infant son born on the voyage.

Others of Billericay followed to New England including a Ralph Hill who was among those to whom can be attributed the founding and naming of Billerica, Massachusetts, in 1655. In fact, when townships were being established in Massachusetts by emigrants largely from the eastern counties of England, as many as three dozen were given East Anglia names.

If it is meaningful to determine what's-in-a-name, St. Mary Magdalen Church on the High Street may be the best place to begin. It is on the site of the Chantry Chapel founded in 1342 in order to accommodate the people of Billericay for whom the parish church located some two miles away was inaccessible. It also served the needs of pilgrims passing through on their way to Canterbury or to the Shrine of our Lady of Walsingham. Lands given to the support of the Chantry and its priest included the manor of Ramsden Crays, from which the name of the town may be derived. Simon de Crais owned the manor in the thirteenth century when it was Vill de Crais. Myriad spellings, including Villdecrey and Billerecrais, hint at an evolution to Billericay in the name. So it is to that conjecture that the American "Billerica" can be traced.

In any case, the chapel was entirely rebuilt in 1490 and has undergone considerable alterations over the years. It was suppressed by Edward VI in 1550 and largely rebuilt in Georgian style in the 1780's. As seen today, the interior is reminiscent of a little New England church, with balcony and characteristic simplicity of style and decor.

New England reminders are appropriate, for just opposite is the Chantry House, on the site of the Chantry priest's house, with its early sixteenth-century paneling, its seventeenth-century fireplace and exposed beams (probably recycled ships' timbers), and its twentieth-century pub. But of greatest significance for New World history, Christopher Martin is said to have lived here.

No English town has charm without its inns and pubs, and Billericay has its share of charm. The Chequers is an old world inn of the sixteenth century, of timber construction, with low ceilings and beams. Located opposite the Chantry House, it undoubtedly entertained and lodged visiting priests among its guests.

The Crown Hotel has been licensed for at least four hundred years, although it is now on its third site. Dick Turpin, that infamous highwayman born in Essex in 1705, is associated with Billericay, specifically with the Crown Inn. Here he is supposed to have ridden his horse up the staircase, in anticipation of the American Western, and jumped out of an upstairs window to make his escape. Naturally, his ghost still rides Billericay roads.

Returning to more sober ideas, off Chapel Street is Mayflower Hall, built in 1920 by the Congregational Church to commemorate the tercentenary of the Pilgrim Fathers. A plaque in the entrance establishes the part played by Billericay in the Mayflower venture. The Congregational Church itself is nearby.

But Billericay is more than just a source for Americana. Archeological evidence exists of man's presence here in the Stone Age. There is evidence too of a prehistoric hill-fort settlement. In a later era, the site was a Roman villa. Billericay had a market in the thirteenth century and two fairs; hence it was an important and thriving town in the Middle Ages. On the unspoiled main street are preserved a number of buildings of interest, a few dating to the fifteenth century. Fine Georgian houses are preserved as well—all attesting to a prosperous past.

The Cater Museum is concerned with the history of Billericay from the Iron Age. Its collection consists of a diversity and profusion of displays such as English coins of the twelfth century, rooms furnished in authentic Victorian fashion, fragments of a German Zeppelin shot down in the area in 1916. Among the maps, sketches, data, and information illustrating the town's history is a photograph of Billerica in Massachusetts.

So it would seem that American associations are dominant. The Chantry House was, until very recently, a fine English restaurant with such traditional specialities on the menu as Pork Mayflower and Petit Poussin

Pilgrim. However, "Ye Olde Chantry" has now been replaced by the "Indian Restaurant." This would seem to be one case where the Indians won out over the Pilgrims.

The Chantry House

Boston

Old Boston in England is, naturally, a popular pilgrimage for Americans. Indeed, the stranger in Boston is soon made overtly aware of ties to the Massachusetts namesake. American accents can be heard everywhere, American addresses can be read with surprising frequency in various visitors' registers, and the American flag may even be seen flying on several buildings.

If the visit is undertaken as a pilgrimage to the past, to the source of new Boston, the tour could appropriately start in the old Guildhall. Inside the fifteenth-century Guildhall are the iron-gated cells which once imprisoned seven "offenders" including William Bradford and William Brewster. The group, later to be known as the Pilgrim Fathers, was betrayed by the captain of a Dutch ship and arrested as they attempted to sail in 1607 from Boston to Holland and thence to the New World. They were tried in the courtroom above the cells. A more successful attempt followed in 1630, and the settlement established was named "Boston" to commemorate the associations which were so meaningful to the Massachusetts colonists.

But the naming of old Boston in Lincolnshire goes back to the year 654 when a considerate and popular Benedictine monk named St. Botolph requested a site in the uninhabited, desolate fenland in order not to evict residents from lands they possessed. When his monastery was destroyed by the Danes in 870, it was rebuilt and the area called St. Botolph's Town. From that tribute to its founder, the name can be traced to the contracted and corrupted form in present usage.

Boston today, with a population over 26,000 is a prosperous country town situated in a highly productive agricultural area. Situated also on the River Witham, Boston is a busy port and a center for a thriving shell fish industry. That and the surrounding Fen country, characterized by stretches of watery fields, recall our own Boston. (No wonder a certain area in the marshy Back Bay came to be called the Fenway.) It was largely in the eighteenth century that huge areas of the Fens were drained by canals and dykes and man-made watercourses and enclosed for farming purposes. The centrally located Market Place, with its stalls selling fresh produce, serves as a perennial reminder of agricultural yield. As a further extension of crop production, the canning of fruits and vegetables is a major Boston industry. But this is not a modern trafficked city, for there in the center of downtown Boston, in Willoughby Street, is a windmill. The Maud Foster windmill, unusual for its five sails or sweeps, was built in 1809 to grind corn. It is still in working order and remains a fine example of just one of the many mills which once abounded.

Among many other Dutch associations and influences is a thriving tulip bulb industry. Over 10,000 acres of tulip fields in Lincolnshire rival those in Holland for production and beauty and are worth a visit in the springtime. One area of the county, to the southeast, is even called Holland for the reason that it too can be characterized as hollow or flat land.

But one need not leave the center of the town to enjoy the pleasant impression of Boston itself, which is conveyed in the area around the irregularly-shaped Market Place. The architectural variety and charm can be seen all around in such buildings as the Grand Peacock and Royal Hotel of about 1670 or the Exchange buildings dated 1772 or the Assembly Rooms of 1826 with Tuscan columns and tall windows lighting a large assembly room.

Colorful though the area may be on market days, the scene is dominated, as it has been for centuries, by the enormous St. Botolph's Church with its fine soaring lantern tower, affectionately known to all as the "Stump." This prodigious parish church is 282 feet long and 100 feet wide with a tower that rises to a height of 272 feet.

Why the exceedingly high tower is called the Stump no one knows. But the tradition of the name may be the best evidence that a spire was originally intended to top the whole. Perhaps it reflects modesty of Bostonians. Or perhaps it was the envious expression of neighbors, for a claustrophobic climb to the first balcony of the tower can give some remarkable views of the town and fenland—one third of the county—including, on a clear day, Lincoln Cathedral, some thirty miles off. The ascender can look down at the red roofs and confused maze of streets or follow the course of the Witham or look northwards to the Lincolnshire of Tennyson's childhood.

In fact, the open stonework gives this medieval lantern tower a rather fragile appearance for its practical function. Designed to act as a guide to mariners out at sea and to travelers who would see it across the Fens, it obviates any idea of originality attributed to the new Boston patriots who used a lantern in the Old North Church steeple as a warning guide: "One if by land and two if by sea. . . ."

Inside, the tower again makes an unforgettable impression as it opens up to a height of 137 feet. American associations pile up too. In the tower area, is a memorial to five Boston men who later became governors of Massachusetts. Ironically, the need for repairs is one of the ties that binds the two Bostons. In 1931, Americans donated a generous sum for restoration of the tower. And earlier, in 1857, the people of Boston,

Boston Stump

Massachusetts, were responsible for restoring one of the former guild chapels in memory of John Cotton, who was vicar of St. Botolph's from 1612 until he left for the other Boston in 1631.

Renovations and changes, which have been going on continually, tie the two Bostons in both directions. Tracery from one chancel window in the east end was removed and shipped across the ocean to be installed in a cloister at Trinity Church in Copley Square, Boston.

Begun in 1309, St. Botolph's Church was completed nearly one hundred

13

years later, only to have rebuilding start all over again. With thirty feet of soft silt underneath, the foundations caused pillars in the east to lean. Various repairs had to be undertaken in the east bay which was extended to include a new roof; the chancel was lengthened by two bays to increase stability of the building. Amazingly, there has been no problem with the foundation since. It may be mere coincidence rather than tradition that a certain towering building in new Boston developed structural difficulties upon completion; perhaps it too will be blessed with a long life.

The reason for the enormous size of St. Botolph's can be attributed to the equally enormous prosperity which the town achieved in the fourteenth century. Its position on the east coast established Boston as an important port as early as 1204, when King John granted its charter. Trade boomed and by the middle of the fourteenth century, Boston was second only to London as the busiest port in the country. Wool was the chief export. Hanseatic merchants became well established, and prosperous guilds paid for the building of the church. However, the wool trade did not survive. Boston began a sad decline first with a series of plagues and then in the early fifteenth century when floods caused the silting up of the river. As a direct result of the great flood of 1571, Boston became a distressed area. The town rallied again, particularly after the drainage of the northern Fens, but the prosperity of the eighteenth century was only moderate in comparison. The disproportionately giant church remains as a symbol of former prosperity brought about by the wealthy wool trade. Significantly, the steeple faces the river, as if looking toward the port and source of Boston's wealth—the reason for its existence.

In the immensely attractive and famous town of Boston, ruins as well as splendid buildings survive to look back at history. Friars settled here, as they did in all thriving medieval towns, but only remains are to be found now of Blackfriars, in Spain Lane, once part of the thirteenth-century Dominican friary and now converted into a theatre.

The Guildhall, of course, serves as a well-preserved and poignant reminder of the past. Just next to it is the Fydell House, built in 1726, predictably by William Fydell, a successful wine merchant who was also three times mayor of Boston. It is a superb town house and an excellent example of eighteenth-century domestic architecture. One room, opened in 1938 by the American ambassador, the Hon. Joseph P. Kennedy, has been designated for the use of American visitors from Boston, Massachusetts. Here, the pilgrim may pause to rest or to ponder the past. American identity and Boston beginnings are everywhere. Consider this final curiosity: Just eight miles away is a place, a hamlet actually, called Bunker's Hill.

14

Braintree

The intersection of the old Roman road from Colchester to St. Albans, one of the busiest in the land, and from London to Bury St. Edmunds made a natural choice for the establishment of the town now known as Braintree. The earlier "Branchetreu" meant simply "town near a river." Here, the tribal chieftain Cunobelin, Shakespeare's Cymbeline, had reigned up to the time of the Roman invasion. When Roman rule ceased after over three hundred years, the area was occupied by the East Saxons, who gave their name to the county of Essex. With a favorable position in north Essex, between the rivers Brain and Pant, some forty miles from London, the steady growth of Braintree was insured.

In 1199 Braintree was granted a charter by King John to allow the holding of a weekly market, a market which insured the town's position as center of the district. It still flourishes today, on Wednesdays, in, naturally enough, Market Square.

The number of ancient inns extant serve as a reminder of those times when pilgrims stopped in Braintree en route to shrines at Bury St. Edmunds or Walsingham. The "Angel" sign, in Notley Road, imposes modern humor in its depiction of winged angel with foaming pint, but it is the pint of beer which has earned the halo. Pilgrim traffic contributed to the growth of Braintree. So did the woolen industry.

Pub Sign in Braintree

A cloth weaving industry, particularly of fine wool, was established in nearby Bocking early in the fourteenth century. One clothier's house in Bradford Street, now called Tudor House, has been restored and opened as a museum and relic of the active woolen cloth manufacture of medieval

15

Tudor House Museum

times. By 1389, silk weaving was established as well, and Braintree has been noted as a cloth-producing center ever since. Through changes in techniques, through waves of depression and unemployment—through centuries—Braintree has remained a textile town. Today, it is dominated by the huge Courtauld works which began here in 1816, having developed from a small family silk business into the world-known synthetic fabric manufacturing concern.

Ancient government was served by a body of twenty-four citizens known as the "Four and Twenty." Although the origins of this little oligarchy are unknown, the services of this undemocratic governing body lasted over a century, from at least 1565 to their final disappearance in 1716. According to just one of many theories which abound, they are known to us in the old nursery rhyme of "four and twenty blackbirds baked in a pie." It's a far cry from that government to the present administrative setup which has merged the contiguous parish of Bocking with Braintree into a single unit. This must be a sensible and practical idea, for based on thirteenth-century accounts, pilgrims were just as uncertain as contemporary travelers where one ended and the other began.

There are some ancient houses, particularly in the Bocking area, but Braintree gives the impression of a busy, modern town. The Town Hall, in the Market Square, was built in 1928 on the site of a field on which William Pygot, a Protestant martyr, was burned at the stake on March 28, 1555. The Council Chamber of the Town Hall has been decorated with murals

16

depicting major events in Braintree history, and one mural portrays the victim being asked to recant as brushwood around him is about to be lit. Also inside the Town Hall are reminders of the results of non-conformity on the establishment of Braintree in Massachusetts.

In the entry hall is a model of the Lyon, the ship which carried the "Braintree Company"—actually 350 passengers recruited from various parts of Essex—to the New World in 1632.

A mural on the east wall of the Council Chamber depicts, in greater detail, the sailing of the Braintree contingent. The Reverend Thomas Hooker, originally from Chelmsford, is seen bidding farwell to Dr. William Goodwyn of Bocking. Behind him stands John Bridge of Braintree, who is honored in Cambridge, Massachusetts, by a statue on the Common. Others kneel in prayer for a safe voyage.

The Braintree Company came to an earlier settlement of 1625 made up of indentured servants and called Mt. Wollaston, site of scandalous activities and a dubious past. Thomas Morton was responsible for the setting up of a Maypole at a place dubbed Merrymount. For his notorious Maypole festivities, he was expelled, and the unruly settlers were replaced by the hard-working, serious Braintree immigrants. The Reverend Hooker arrived the following year to join his flock, after having barely escaped summons and arrest by Archbishop Laud for his ardent preaching on Puritanism. But restless Thomas Hooker soon moved to Newetowne (now Cambridge) with many of his followers and, still dissatisfied, left there for the wilderness of Hartford, Connecticut. The remaining settlers first established a church and then established the town, which was incorporated in 1640 and called Braintree.

The Massachusetts city has much in its heritage to be proud of. Among the famous men to come from Braintree are two presidents of the United States, John Adams and his son John Quincy Adams, and John Hancock, President of the Continental Congress.

It is hard to imagine a town with closer, warmer feelings toward its mother town. Braintree, Massachusetts, presented a plaque to the Town Hall of Braintree, Essex, to commemorate the 750th anniversary of the granting of the Braintree Market Charter in 1199.

Also believed to be founded in 1199 is the Church of St. Michael the Archangel. Its tower and east chancel wall include Roman bricks. Most of the nave and tower is work of 1240. It was enlarged in the thirteenth century by the addition of north and south aisles and tower. A century later the nave was heightened by addition of clerestory, and a new roof was built. Changes and renovations have been made continually. Nevertheless the church is a fine building with a handsome tower—a harmonious adaptation of new changes on older traditions. It has literary interest too in the fact that Nicholas Udall, vicar of Braintree from 1537 to 1544 and author of *Ralph Roister Doister*, is believed to have written plays which were performed here.

Braintree is surrounded by attractive villages, but Coggeshall is particularly beautiful and historically important. Located on the Blackwater and on the Roman road from Colchester to St. Albans, it was a major cloth making center in the fifteenth and sixteenth centuries and a center for Tarmbour lace in the nineteenth century. It has the remains of a twelfth-century Cistercian Abbey, the splendid Perpendicular church of St. Peter-ad-Vincula, and the beautiful, timbered, sixteenth-century house of the wealthy clothier, Thomas Paycocke, which is now preserved by the National Trust.

Great Maplestead has a Norman church, and Little Maplestead has a rare circular church (founded in 1340 by the Knights Hospitallers of St. John of Jerusalem), the smallest of five ancient round churches still existing in England. Finchingfield is one of England's most photographed villages, with its seventeenth-century cottages set by the pond and village green, and its church of Norman origins in the background.

But it is easy to reverse completely the tourist process of the taking of photographs. A large album, located in the Braintree Town Hall, was presented on the occasion of the celebration by Braintree, Massachusetts, of its tercentenary in 1940. Among the pictures of interest (such as the Rotary Club, Boy Scouts, Women's Republican Club) is a copy of the deed of purchase of "Braintrey" from the Indians for twenty-one pounds and ten shillings. Thus, instead of taking photographs of Braintree in old England, the visitor can *look* at photos of Braintree in New England.

Brighton

The influx of August visitors to Brighton in England is a reversal of the exodus of August residents *from* Brighton in Massachusetts. The movement in both cases can be attributed in large part to throngs of holiday-bound trippers seeking the pleasures of sunny shore resorts.

The tradition which nurtured the stylish seaside resort of Brighton in Sussex and made it a standard for measuring seaside resorts elsewhere can perhaps be said to emanate from Dr. Richard Russell, the "inventor" of sea bathing. Dr. Russell had been prescribing to his patients the sea-water cure with such enormous success that he moved his practice to Brighton in 1754 to further foster his belief in sea bathing as a health-inducing activity. His prescriptions transformed the poor fishing village of Brighthelmstone into a fashionable watering place. Salubrious sea water, it was proclaimed, could cure a range of diseases from asthma and rheumatism to consumption and cancer. But surely, it must have been its promise to renew sexual prowess and vitality that had no small part in the guaranteed success of this fashionable form of medical therapy.

After Dr. Russell published a thesis, in 1750, on the meritorious effects of sea water—both for bathing in *and* for drinking—Brighthelmstone sea water was bottled and sold in London to those who could not get to Brighton, much as today tins of Cape Cod air are sold, presumably for those who cannot leave their sweltering cities. Dr. Russell's epitaph bears the quotation from Euripides which must have been his motto in life: "The sea washes away all the ills of mankind."

In the early history of this new pastime of sea bathing, a device known as the bathing machine was used. A small shed on wheels served as a dressing room, or more accurately as an undressing room, for men generally wore no bathing costumes at all until about 1865, while women might be clothed in a kind of nightgown. The participant remained in the shed to be immersed as the chariot was drawn out into the water by horses. And perhaps a viewer or two remained on shore, with a telescope, to peruse splashing, naked figures. Brighton never adopted the modest precaution of a canvas hood over the steps of the bathing machine to conceal the bather—a practice that was characteristic of less scandalous shore resorts such as Margate, Weymouth, or Scarborough. By about 1750, attendants known as "dippers" and "bathers" established their personalities on the scene with their function to make certain that their charges were properly immersed.

The fashionable Sussex seaside resort attracted many fashionable visitors

19

Royal Pavilion

over the years. The historian Edward Gibbon came in 1781, just after publication of his third volume of *Decline and Fall of the Roman Empire.* Charles Dickens stayed on several occasions and wrote *Bleak House* and *Dombey and Son* here. Thackeray visited and included a description of "brisk, gay, and gaudy" Brighton in his *Vanity Fair.* Dr. Samuel Johnson was another distinguished visitor. Among the artists are such notables as Sir Joshua Reynolds, John Constable, and J. M. W. Turner.

But it was the arrival of the Prince of Wales in 1783 that was to brighten the character of Brighton and change it irrevocably. From his very first visit, the Prince (later King George IV) was enchanted with the town and returned regularly. The villa that he required was continually enlarged or altered, over a thirty-five year period, to accommodate and reflect his brilliant social life. The ultimate design for Regency revels is credited to the architect John Nash. It was his plan, when the Prince a stately pleasure-dome decreed, that brought about the realization of an oriental fantasy. The English imagination, captivated by Eastern splendors, now had its own splendid rendition in the minarets and pinnacles and onion-shaped domes of the fantastic Royal Pavilion.

Queen Victoria, however, did not find it suitable to her need for privacy, and the Royal Pavilion was sold to the town in 1850. The elegant eccentricities of the entire estate have been a delightful center for the public ever since.

The glass-domed Royal Stables were converted into a concert hall. The riding school, known as Corn Exchange, is used for flower shows and other exhibitions. The former indoor tennis court is the present Art Gallery. But the Royal Pavilion, with its sensational Indian effect, is at the center of the estate and indeed of all that is associated with the panache of Brighton.

The interior of the Royal Pavilion is no less sensational. Among the lavish interior eccentricities which may be viewed and enjoyed are: the Banqueting Room (with exotic plantain tree ceiling and rich dragon decorations), the Kitchen (full of copper pans, roasting spits, and stylized palm tree columns), the Music Room (with stylized lotus-like chandeliers arranged around the circular room), and the King's Apartments (with hidden door leading to a bedroom above).

It is hard to remember that Brighton was not always a gay and sophisticated pleasure resort, that it has a past much older than Regency. In the Brighton Museum are skeletal remains and artifacts from recent archeological excavations giving evidence of the earliest inhabitants of Brighton some five thousand years ago. And a nearby prehistoric hill-fort called Hollingbury Camp further attests to a much earlier civilization.

West Pier

Just as its use as a resort is a relatively modern phenomenon, so its name is a modern adaptation. It seems probable that the name of Brighton, which derives from Brighthelmstone, may be further traced to a St. Brightelm. In one variation of his story, he is an Anglo-Saxon bishop who accompanied the Saxon army and died in battle in 693. The popular and current form of the name came into use around the end of the eighteenth century and into official use in 1810. It seems highly likely that Brighton, Massachusetts, incorporated in 1807, and now part of Boston, was named for that archetype bathing resort because ancestors of several early American settlers came from that area.

Brighton today is a modern residential town, a dormitory for commuters to London, a center of light industry, and an academic mecca which can boast of its University of Sussex, as well as a seaside resort extravagantly equipped with two piers and promenade. A long way from neolithic man are the monolithic traffic jams created by travelers to Xanadu. In a curious reversal, from the legalized speed set in 1896 of fourteen miles an hour (an occasion still commemorated each year by a procession from London to Brighton of pre-1905 cars), motorists today can often average four miles an hour on fine Sunday summer evenings. The traffic congestion problem is inevitable because of its location—London's nearest point on the English Channel, a distance of only fifty miles.

But also because of its location on the Channel, Brighton has never really been free from fear of invasion. Most recently, it has been invaded by

22

modern developments of flats, shops, restaurants, and office buildings. One area, however, known as the Lanes preserves the character of the old town and makes shopping in Brighton a particular and pleasurable attraction. The Lanes are a maze of alleyways, crowded with shops purveying antiques and rare items and retaining the original flavor of seventeenth-century Brighthelmstone fishermen's cottages.

Although Brighton was badly bombed during the War, the Royal Pavilion was not touched because Hitler intended to use it for his personal headquarters. It remains the cynosure and symbol of romantic potentialities. Perhaps the fiction of Jane Austen is indeed reality, as when a character in *Pride and Prejudice* suggests that "a visit to Brighton comprised every possibility of earthly happiness."

Cambridge

Picture this sunny scene: a river setting with punts or sculls plying their way upstream, students reading or relaxing on the grassy embankment—perhaps watching a boat race, perhaps watching joggers—university buildings in the background, attractive footbridges over the river, visitors or shoppers taking a restful break in the friendly atmosphere of what is unquestionably a university town. Cambridge, yes! But which one?

When the American settlement of Newetowne was selected in 1638 by the ministers and leaders of the community, most of whom were educated at Cambridge University, England, to be the new seat of learning, its name was changed—reasonably—to Cambridge. It was expected that the newborn infant would grow and emulate its parent in every way. The college itself was named for a man who bequeathed his entire library at his death in 1638. An American in England wishing to pay homage to John Harvard might visit the Harvard House in Stratford, the early home of his mother, or the Harvard Chapel in Southwark Cathedral, London, where he was baptized. Founded in 1636, the new institution was well on its way toward fulfilling its potential, toward attaining the status of the older counterpart, when John Wilson wrote in 1704:

> And as old Cambridge well deserved the name,
> May the new Cambridge win as pure a fame.

It is not possible to ascertain the origins or precise date of the founding of old Cambridge University. In the twelfth century, the word *universitas* referred merely to an organized body of men, a corporation. Young men simply came in the Middle Ages to the ancient religious houses of greater abbeys to be educated and lodged with a master or in private quarters. What is known is that in 1209 a migration of scholars from Oxford to Cambridge took place. They selected Cambridge perhaps by chance, perhaps by reputation of existing schools and teachers; but a university has been in existence at Cambridge at least from that date.

Peterhouse, the first Cambridge college, was founded in 1284. St. Peter's Church and two neighboring hostels were turned over to Bishop Hugh de Balsham for his body of secular scholars to live together as students of the university. The college was ravaged by fire in the fifteenth century, and hardly any of the original buildings remain. The poet Thomas Gray lived at Peterhouse in 1756, and the iron bar which he fixed to his window on the north side of the main court may still be seen. A rope ladder could be suspended from the bar in case of fire. His phobia made him the unhappy butt of an undergraduate prank. After a false alarm with cries of fire caused him to slide down the rope ladder in his nightshirt and into a tub of cold water, Gray transferred to Pembroke, across the road.

King's College was founded by Henry VI in 1441. Its many fine features are dominated by one of the most magnificent examples of Perpendicular architecture in England—King's College Chapel. A very large area of brilliantly colored glass gives the feeling of lightness to the vaulted roof. Thus the poet John Betjeman describes the network of tracery and fan vaulting: "With what rich precision the stonework soars and springs to

King's College Chapel

25

fountain out a spreading vault—a shower that never falls." When the voices of the world-famous choir of King's College Chapel fill the void, the result is inspirational. Wordsworth's sonnet speaks of

> that branching roof
> Self-poised, and scooped into ten thousand cells,
> Where light and shade repose, where music dwells
> Lingering—and wandering on as loth to die;
> Like thoughts whose very sweetness yieldeth proof
> That they were born for immortality.

Adding to the riches of the chapel is *The Adoration of the Magi* of Rubens which forms the altar-piece. No, it is not possible to assimilate the splendors in one brief visit. A member of the chapel staff recalls an American couple who explained that they had flown to England just to visit King's College Chapel, Cambridge. They gazed at the lofty vault and ecstatically left after a two-day jaunt across the Atlantic, having paid the ultimate tribute.

Queens' was founded by two queens, Margaret of Anjou and Elizabeth Woodville. Queen Margaret founded it in 1448 while her husband, Henry VI, was busy with the founding of King's. Her purpose was to honor women. The need to educate them was not appreciated until 1869 with the establishment of Girton, a college for women. Edward IV's queen, Elizabeth Woodville, took over the sponsorship in 1465 after the defeat of Henry VI in the Wars of the Roses. Her portrait hangs in the hall behind the president's chair. The Cloister Court which she built is one of the most beautiful in Cambridge; a spectacular Tudor building on the north side of the court is the half-timbered President's Lodge. In the southwest corner of the Principal Court is Erasmus's Tower, aptly named since that is where the great humanist stayed when he was at Queens'. The wooden Mathematical Bridge, built in 1749 without a single nail, gives a fine view of the college.

Trinity is the largest. Henry VIII founded it in 1546, a year before his death. His statue is on one side of the Great Gate. In the Hall, which has a fine hammerbeam roof, is a famous portrait of Henry VIII by Holbein. The Wren Library with carvings by Grinling Gibbons is a treasured attraction both for its architectural design and for its contents. To Trinity belong such names as Dryden, Byron, Macaulay, Tennyson, Housman, Sir Isaac Newton, and John Winthrop of New England fame.

St. John's, the second largest in Cambridge, has a magnificent turreted gatehouse, a splendid Tudor hall with hammerbeam roof, and an enclosed bridge with traceried windows over the River Cam, the famous Bridge of Sighs, named for the one in Venice.

Magdalen contains the library bequeathed to it by Samuel Pepys. In the

Bridge of Sighs, St. John's College

Pepysian Library, among some three thousand books of value and interest, was discovered the famous Diary which was later transcribed from the shorthand of the author's private system and published in 1825.

In the famous garden of Christ's College is the mulberry tree which makes it famous, for it is associated with a student of renown who was at Christ's from 1625 to 1632. John Milton is said to have written *Lycidas* under this legendary tree.

Founded in 1497 on the site of a Benedictine nunnery, Jesus College has many old and beautiful bits of architecture, especially the thirteenth-century St. Radegund's Church, now the chapel of the college and updated with stained-glass windows by Burne-Jones. In the library of Jesus is the first edition of the first Bible ever printed in America—in fact, in Cambridge. A Jesus man, John Eliot, whose mission it was to convert the Indians, had it printed in 1663 in the language of the Mohicans.

Emmanuel was one of the later colleges. Founded in 1584, it was a strongly Puritan college and the source of many emigrants to America, including John Harvard. A window to the memory of John Harvard was placed in the Wren Chapel in 1884, at the tercentenary celebration.

It is not possible to uncover all that Cambridge has, not even if one lives there. Beyond college gateways are peaceful courts, beautiful gardens, and

27

quiet cloisters, all enhancing those fine examples of college architecture. The area between the big colleges and the River Cam is known as the "Backs" and is a great delight, particularly to picture takers or to paddlers who may hire boats. The forty acres of Botanical Gardens had as its original purpose to show uses of plants in medicine. Museums abound, and the Fitzwilliam Museum is one of the finest in the country. Its collections of paintings, engravings, books, and other valuables should keep a visitor enthralled for many, many days at least.

Colleges and college life dominate, but the city is much older than its university. Because of its site, Cambridge had to be important. Located on the River Cam, it provided the only good possibility for crossing by means of a ford and later a bridge. Around the hard ground which became Cambridge, stretched the undrained fenlands—swamps, streams, and lakes—which separated East Anglia from the rest of the country. Thus, Cambridge was an oasis even some two thousand years ago.

When a Roman fort was established in A.D. 43, it replaced an earlier settlement. Clearly, the Romans appreciated the need to guard the fort from a position on the high ground to the west of the river which they knew as the Granta. By the second century, the Roman town had a grid pattern of streets, and Roman roads passed through or near Cambridge.

Danish invaders occupied, in 875, the town called Granta Bridge (by then the ford was bridged) and made it their local army headquarters in 921. The ever-changing name evolved from Grantebrige, Cantebrigg, Cauntebrigg, and Caumbridge to its modern form, which came into use in the sixteenth century.

In the tenth and eleventh centuries, Cambridge was very important because of its location at the head of a river, with access to the sea via King's Lynn, and as a point of communication between East Anglia and the rest of England. The Church of St. Benet was built in this period, and the original tower of 1025 is still standing—the oldest building in town and one of the most complete Anglo-Saxon buildings in the country. The church is connected to Corpus Christi College by a sixteenth-century brick passageway.

All that remains of the castle built by William in 1068 after the Norman Conquest is the mound on Castle Hill.

The Round Church, the Church of the Holy Sepulchre, of the early twelfth century, is the oldest of five round churches extant in England. Its design was based on the plan of the Holy Sepulchre in Jerusalem and influenced by the returning crusaders.

Great St. Mary's in King's Parade is the university church, and its tower is well worth climbing for a great view of Cambridge.

Little St. Mary's, near Peterhouse, is a little gem which contains the interesting monument to Godfrey Washington. The stars-and-stripes coat of arms of this clergyman recalls the American flag given by a well-known member of his family.

Not limiting itself to history, Cambridge even has a wonderful bit of lore attached to it which involves Thomas Hobson. This wealthy town figure, many times mayor, kept forty horses in his livery stable for hire by a system of rotation. A customer could hire any horse, provided it was the one Hobson chose. When he died in 1630, the phrase "Hobson's Choice" was destined for immortality.

Cantabrigians on both sides would surely agree that Cambridge is inexhaustible and that, taking both sides into account, Cambridge must be one of the best known and prestigious names in the world.

The Washington Memorial in Little St. Mary's

29

Chelmsford

The English Chelmsford, as its name suggests, was situated on a fordable part of the river Chelmer. Recorded history traces Chelmsford back to the middle of the first century when it was the site of the Roman Caesaromagus.

Actually, two rivers, the Can and the Chelmer, divided the town into three sections. When Maurice, Bishop of London, built the first bridge over the river Can in about 1100 during the reign of Henry I, the town inevitably increased in importance and never really stopped growing. By 1189 Chelmsford was the assize town. By 1200 it had a market and a fair. So vital was the change, that in the Coat of Arms is a representation of that historic bridge of three arches. The present Stone Bridge dates from 1787.

Situated just 29 miles from London, and just a half hour train journey away, Chelmsford has developed into an industrial center with several important factories. In particular, it is the birthplace of the radio industry. A company formed by Marconi started operations here in 1897. After successfully spanning the Atlantic by wireless signal in 1901, expansion was rapid. Today there is concentration on all sorts of electronic equipment dealing with broadcasting and telecommunications.

Nevertheless, this cathedral town and county town of Essex manages to maintain antiquities and characteristics which make it very special. The Chelmsford and Essex Museum, in a Victorian mansion of Oaklands Park in Moulsham Street, contains such varied displays as Bronze Age implements, huge Roman vase found at Maldon, medieval English arts, one thousand British birds, and a picture gallery which includes a Turner and landscapes by Constable and Gainsborough.

The contrasting and bustling flow of contemporary life is in the town center with its busy stores and offices, new pedestrian shopping center, buildings of architectural interest, and bits of old history. On the High Street near Tindal Square is the Saracen's Head, where Anthony Trollope worked on his novels. Sir Nicholas Tindal is honored by his statue in the Square. Born in Chelmsford in 1776, this local boy made good by working his way up to finally become a Chief Justice before he died in 1846.

But there is a memorial of another kind to a local boy who made good in America. Thomas Hooker, a minister of Chelmsford, who later left for Braintree, emigrated to New England at about the time of the Pilgrim Fathers. The Reverend Thomas Hooker had been curate of St. Mary's in the English Chelmsford, and the American Chelmsford was named for its older counterpart, the home of early settlers.

Tindal Square

The church in which the Reverend Thomas Hooker had been minister, now a cathedral, is almost hidden behind shops along Tindal Square and overshadowed by offices of County Hall. The fifteenth-century parish church of St. Mary the Virgin, St. Peter and St. Cedd attained cathedral status in 1914 when Essex became a separate ecclesiastical diocese. It is a typical Essex parish church of the Perpendicular style and rectangular plan of the fifteenth century. Its tower shows Norman traces, although it was rebuilt in 1424. In the north wall of the chancel is a unique fifteenth-century fan arch. There are seventeenth-century Dutch altar rails. Much that is new includes the Bishop's throne (1922), life-size statue of the first Bishop of Chelmsford, John Edwin Watts-Ditchfield (1931), high altar (1931), and medieval-style coloring of the sanctuary and chancel roof (1957). A modern St. Peter is outside on the southeast corner, a modern fisherman holding an ordinary modern house key. The porch was beautifully restored in 1953 as a memorial to United States airmen stationed in Essex in World War II. Stained glass represents the seal of the United States of America, and of the United States Air Force, as well as the Washington family arms; the great-great-grandfather of George Washington was an Essex clergyman. The

31

inscription in the glass explains that the porch was "enriched and beautified by Essex friends of the American people" and indicates a continuous friendship.

Chelmsford is within easy reach of London and within easier reach of beautiful little villages. The unspoiled village of Little Writtle, two miles west of Chelmsford, with its old houses set around a triangular green with a pond at the apex, is perhaps the most tranquil. Surprisingly, it was more important than Chelmsford at the time of Domesday; but when the bridge was built in Chelmsford, the highway was diverted and so was Writtle's prosperity.

Ingatestone, six miles southwest on the Chelmsford-London Road, is a pleasant village with a sixteenth-century inn and a fine mansion. Ingatestone Hall, as it is known, was erected in 1565 by Sir William Petre who acquired the estate at the time of the Dissolution of the Monasteries. Elizabeth I was lavishly entertained there. And William Byrd, the Elizabethan composer, was a frequent visitor. One of its features is a priest's hiding hole concealed in an upper story. The house was the setting for the novel, *Lady Audley's Secret* by Mary Elizabeth Braddon.

Yet Chelmsford, because of its location within easy access of London, inevitably gets the spillover from London. It is a commuter's community like its American counterpart, which is also within easy access of the big city. If that similarity were not striking enough to call up images of New England, road signs point to such familiar names as Springfield, Waltham, Billericay, Maldon, and Braintree.

St. Peter on Southeast Corner of Chelmsford Cathedral

Dartmouth

The old and picturesque town of Dartmouth, situated on a hillside just inside the mouth of the lovely River Dart, has a magnificent, sheltered, deep-water harbor and a dramatic setting on the South Devon coast of the English Channel.

The town began life in the twelfth century. From here, the Second Crusade departed in 1147; and the Third Crusade, led by Richard the Lion Heart, in 1190. But the most recent and largest gathering for a military operation occurred in 1944 when 485 ships of the United States Navy used this important taking-off position for the Normandy invasion.

Long before this modern crusade, in medieval times, the town grew rich on piracy, privateering, and a thriving wine trade with Bordeaux. Chaucer visited Dartmouth in 1373 as a customs officer and is believed to have met John Hawley, an importer of French wine and the greatest of all merchants and shipmasters of that thriving medieval port. He may be the wily character alluded to by Chaucer in *The Canterbury Tales*:

> A Shipman was ther, wonyng fer by weste
> For aught I woot he was of Dertemouthe.

Elizabethan and Jacobean houses can still be seen on the quay and elsewhere to testify to the town's wealthy past. The Butterwalk is a particularly appealing architectural gem. The seventeenth-century colonnaded row houses consist of shops below and timbered living quarters above, which, supported by granite columns, project out over the sidewalk. Number 12, now a chemist's shop, has a fine plaster ceiling of the Tree of Jesse; Number 10 is the Butterwalk Restaurant. The Borough Museum is at Number 6. Built in the reign of Charles I in the 1630's, the Butterwalk was restored after enemy bombing during the War caused some destruction.

Dartmouth's location gave it a significant role in the exploration and settlement of the New World. Among the explorers based here at some point in their careers were Sir Walter Raleigh, Humphrey and Adrian Gilbert, and John Davis.

On the cobbled quay known as Bayard's Cove is a monument to what is perhaps the best-known voyage of exploration. The Pilgrim Fathers paid an unexpected visit to Dartmouth in August 1620 for eight days of repairs to the Speedwell. Apparently the work done was inadequate because the Speedwell and its accompanying ship, the Mayflower, had to put in again at Plymouth for further repairs. (The Speedwell was eventually abandoned.)

The Butterwalk

Thus, the town was deprived of the opportunity of being immortalized in the New World with a "Dartmouth Rock."

Near the quay is the Church of St. Saviour, notable for its fifteenth-century screen with intricately carved friezes and the elaborately carved fifteenth-century stone pulpit on a slender pillar. One of the best memorial brasses in the country is in the chancel; John Hawley who died in 1408 is depicted in armour with his two wives, Joan and Alice, on either side.

From the quayside, an excursion can be taken from the estuary of the River Dart to Totnes, a twelve-mile journey. The trip goes past sleepy villages with names such as Dittisham and Stoke Gabriel. Points of interest

34

along the route include the Royal Naval College (which has been training naval officers since 1905), the large shipyard at Noss Point, the Greenway House home of the late Agatha Christie, and Sandridge House built by John Nash in 1805.

Dartmouth Castle was built in the 1480's in the reign of Henry VII. It faces a similar castle on the opposite shore across the estuary at Kingswear. The twin castles were designed to guard the narrow entrance by a thick iron chain that could be stretched across the river to prevent enemy ships from entering. Kingswear Castle is now a ruin and not open to the public, but Dartmouth Castle remains very much as it was when Henry VIII, fearing an attack from the Continent, further strengthened the town's defenses in 1537.

The Church of St. Petrox stands next to the Castle. It is a simple seventeenth-century building, bare and without chancel or transepts but with a Norman font and a plethora of tablets and brasses. Together with Dartmouth Castle, it forms an impressive scene on the west side of the Dart.

In the tropical Royal Avenue Gardens near the quay is a monument to Thomas Newcomen (1663-1729) of Dartmouth who invented the first practical steam engine, used in mining districts including the West Country tin mines. The Museum next to the Gardens, as if to atone for the slipshod technology committed on the Speedwell, is dedicated to this Founder of the Industrial Revolution. On view is one of his original atmospheric pumping engines of 1725, the oldest in the world.

Rich in history, architecture, and pubs, this delightful Devon town invites the meanderer to wander and take in the history and the pleasures of a most satisfying town. When Daniel Defoe visited in 1724, he was displeased by its "meanly-built" aspect and pleased by the price of lobsters. A modern traveler would undoubtedly reverse the criticism.

Dedham

Dedham is a Saxon name derived from settlers named Dydd or Dydda, whose "ham" was a clearing by the ford at a time when the River Stour was still unbridged. Other names in Dedham can be less reliable. Castle House, for instance, was a clothier's residence in a town which never had a castle. Now open to the public, the house displays the works of its former owner, the twentieth-century painter and sculptor, Sir Alfred Munnings.

But it is in no way misleading to apply all of the synonyms of "charm" to Dedham, one of the best-looking villages in East Anglia. Essentially a one-street village, with Mill Lane branching off toward the mill and the River Stour, its High Street is lined with ancient and delightful buildings that serve as proof that Dedham was an important and prosperous wool center from the fifteenth to the seventeenth centuries. The Marlborough Head Inn of about 1500 is on the Mill Lane corner of the High Street. The Sun Inn is another early sixteenth-century timber-framed building on the High Street, with carriageway and picturesque stable yard.

Sherman's, High Street

Among the early Georgian brick houses which line the High Street, Sherman's, just opposite the parish church, implies a connection with the wool trade in its name, formerly Shearman. The Grammar School, in the square adjoining the church, is another fine brick building dating from the

Southfields

early eighteenth century. But dating to 1500 is a particularly interesting group of timber-framed dwellings known as Southfields and located about three hundred yards south of the High Street, past the church and the playing fields. This clothier's house consists of the residence quarters of the master weaver as well as the dwellings of his workmen, offices and warehouse, arranged around an interior courtyard.

But the attraction of Dedham, and indeed of the entire area, is the parish Church of St. Mary the Virgin begun in the year in which Columbus discovered America. It was a time of prosperity, when Dedham was becoming an important textile center, and a new church replaced the earlier Saxon or Norman building. St. Mary's is one of the outstanding churches of East Anglia. Built in the Perpendicular style, with a tower 131 feet high, it is situated with its 170-foot-long side to the High Street. Its immense size and its attractive and characteristic use of flint reflect the prosperity brought about by the weaving industry.

The long nave of St. Mary's has a clerestory and a pleasantly decorated ceiling. Among the boss ornaments in the nave ceiling, at the point of intersection of roof beams, is a shield of Dedham in Massachusetts and one of the Commonwealth of Massachusetts. Many left from Dedham in

37

England to help found the colony of Massachusetts Bay, and reminders of the connection between the two Dedhams recur.

The Sherman window in the north aisle is of special American interest. The initials "E.S." belong to Edmund Sherman, a direct ancestor of General W. T. Sherman of American Civil War fame. Edmund Sherman is buried in the churchyard near to this window; the house he lived in still stands across the street—Sherman's Hall. A first cousin of "E.S.," Samuel Sherman, emigrated to Massachusets in 1634. He settled with his family in a place called Contentment, later renamed Dedham.

In the Lady Chapel, in addition to the fourteenth-century piscina, is a pew honoring the people of Dedham, Massachusetts, who contributed generously in 1967 toward restoration of this church. The bench end shows the seal of the Republic—thirteen stars and thirteen arrows in eagle's claw, signifying the thirteen original states. Carved panels on the back of the pew are decorated with various relationships between the two Dedhams including a design of two intertwined D's, the first house of worship in Massachusetts, and the Mayflower.

American associations are brought up to date by an inscription on the first pew of the north side commemorating an event which took place on the twentieth of July, 1969—man's first moon landing.

Wealthy clothiers had built the magnificent church. Again, leading citizens established a Lectureship at Dedham in 1578. This was to be the place for sermons resounding with religious zeal, through a lecture preached on Sunday afternoons and in the hour preceding Tuesday market day.

John Rogers was called to the Dedham Lectureship in 1605. He had been Vicar of Haverhill where he acquired a reputation for his pulpit outpourings. Now he made the Tuesday Lecture at Dedham a county event. His eloquence drew huge audiences and earned him the title of "Roaring Rogers." When he died in 1636, so many people came to pay tribute at the funeral service, that the overcrowded gallery collapsed. He is buried in the parish church, and his monument is against the north wall of the chancel, a half figure within a canopy, looking very much like the Shakespeare monument in Stratford.

Dedham never recovered from the depression it suffered in the 1640's due to a decline in the wool trade, exacerbated by the Civil War and the plague. It had been a thriving industrial community specializing in bays and says, the finer fabrics in contrast with coarser English cloth. Gone is the wealth from wool. But it remains rich in beauty.

Its beauty has been immortalized by John Constable, for Dedham is in Constable country. The master was born in 1776 in nearby East Bergholt on the Suffolk side of the Stour. Dedham is in Essex just two hundred yards from the Suffolk border. The scenes on the banks of the Stour, John Constable said, made him a painter. The Dedham church tower is a favorite subject and can be seen in his *Dedham Mill, Vale of Dedham,* and *A View of the Stour.* So impressed was he with the tower, that he painted it in even where it didn't belong. *The Cornfield*, in the National Gallery, portrays the lane leading from East Bergholt across the meadows to Dedham, but the church seen in the distance is artistic license.

In 1821, he painted his masterpiece, *The Haywain*, also in the National Gallery. In that year, he wrote a letter to his wife from the Old Mill House in Mill Lane where he was staying with his sister, expressing the wish "that we had a small house here." So might any visitor well express the same wish. For although Dedham has lost its former prosperity, it has retained something more meaningful: it has inherited a rich abundance of splendid old buildings and a setting which continues to be a source of inspiration and natural wealth.

Dorchester

So realistically did Thomas Hardy paint the Dorset landscape in his novels, that it is not amiss for a tourist, intrigued by his treatment, to arrive in Dorchester and make the self-congratulatory observation, "I'm here at last—in Casterbridge." That was the name chosen to represent Dorchester in his novels. Hardy also emphasized the dominant feeling of Dorchester when he wrote in *The Mayor of Casterbridge*:

> It announced old Rome in every street, alley and precinct. It looked Roman, bespoke the art of Rome and concealed the dead men of Rome. It was impossible to dig more than a foot or two deep about the town's fields and gardens without coming upon some tall soldier or other of the Empire who had lain in his silent unobtrusive rest for the space of fifteen hundred years.

After the Roman invasion in 43 A.D., the town flourished and took on characteristics that still impart to Dorchester that special antique flavor. Excavations go on continuously, and Roman graves and relics are uncovered frequently. One famous hoard was found in 1936 on the site of the equally famous Marks and Spencer department store in South Street. A Roman necropolis is near Fordington Hill. Other large ones are near South Walks and Salisbury Walks and at Poundbury. Often, it is just the Roman idea or feeling that exists under or through the modern covering. For instance, the thriving Roman town had a main highway (Via Iceniana) with streets branching off from it and houses placed in the rectangular blocks. The public buildings, Forum, and Temple were in the center, around the area of St. Peter's. A careful study of modern Dorchester can reveal the square outline by which the Romans laid out the town in typical grid pattern.

Ruins abound. Existing fragments of Roman walls, twenty-eight feet long, are on the east side of Albert Road. Part of the Roman aqueduct which carried the water supply from Maiden Newton (Chalk Newton in *Tess of the D'Urbervilles*) to Dorchester may also still be seen.

For further traces of Old Rome one could do worse than to visit the fine Dorset County Museum where, amidst the archeological finds, is one skeleton with a Roman dart embedded in its spine.

But evidence of the presence of man in the area goes well beyond the Roman era, some four thousand years back to Neolithic times. Again, the Museum traces the history of the area from the Stone Age to the twentieth century. But even prehistoric remains are all around and not limited merely to the confines of a museum.

Maumbury Rings is a sight which scans the centuries. Originally a Sacred Circle of the late Stone Age, it was converted by the Romans to an amphitheatre in which gladiatorial combats could be seen by a crowd of thirteen thousand. In the Middle Ages it was used for bull- and bear-baiting and for cock-fighting. Then it became an execution site. In modern times, it is a remarkable memorial to the distant past.

Maiden Castle is a gigantic prehistoric hill-fort. It was Mai Dun, the Fortress by the Plain. Situated two miles southwest of Dorchester, and built originally as a defense, this now-dead city is generally accepted as the finest example in the world of a hill fortress. It occupies 120 acres, extends 1000 yards, and has a width of 500 yards.

Another spectacular prehistoric sight is the Cerne Giant, a figure cut into the chalk hill overlooking the beautiful little town of Cerne Abbas, eight miles from Dorchester. An abbey was founded in this town (as its name implies) by St. Augustine in 603. But it was destroyed at the time of the Dissolution, and present monastic remains include only the guest house, tithe barn, and gate house with beautiful two-storied oriel window over the doorway. However, the far more ancient Giant, a huge primitive man holding a club, is probably of late Neolithic date. He stands 186 feet high, covers one acre of ground, and is the subject of great conjectures by great authorities. He is undoubtedly connected with pagan rites. He may be a fertility god, but the absolute certainty of his secret is lost in antiquity.

The long barrows built by people of the late Stone Age for burial of the dead are plentiful in Dorset.

Dorchester was the tribal capital of the Durotriges when the Romans invaded in 43 A.D. They gave to this site of modern Dorchester the Latinized name of "Durnovaria," retaining the root "Durno" which means "a fist" in the ancient language of the Britons. The somewhat puzzling etymology of the name is explained by the authorities as possibly suggesting the shape of the landscape with its hill-fort. It may have looked like a fist. The Saxon settlers added *ceaster* to the Romano-British root, implying that they found it to be the site of a Roman camp or station. Cities as well as their names evolve, and this one turns up in Domesday Book as "Dorecestre."

Through the centuries, the town had its share of plagues, wars, and other disasters. The history of Dorchester in the seventeenth century must have been particularly grim, with the Civil War for one thing. Then, after the Monmouth Rebellion, at the Bloody Assize of 1685, Judge Jeffreys was sent to Dorchester to punish the rebels. Of the 300 prisoners who were tried, 292 were sentenced to death. The infamous Judge Jeffreys lodged in a house in High West Street, now a restaurant. Naturally, stories abound of

41

Church of St. Peter

Dorchester people hearing the ghost of Jeffreys furiously stomping about in those lodgings.

Hardly had the town recovered from the serious plague of 1595 which killed a substantial portion of the population, when, on August 6, 1613, fire burned a large part of the town, including two of its three existing churches. Fire, an ever-present threat, again damaged the town in 1622 and 1775. But the Church of St. Peter, with links to the Roman past and American future, survived. Built on a site believed to be a Roman Temple, the Church has relevance to early American history and is a bright spot of seventeenth-century Dorchester history, certainly for Americans.

It was the Reverend John White, Rector of St. Peter's Church, who promoted colonization of Massachusetts. The "Patriarch of Dorchester" died in 1648 and is buried in St. Peter's. The last line of his epitaph reads: "He greatly set forward the Emigration to the Massachusetts Bay Colony, where his name lives in unfading remembrance."

Although he did not himself join any expedition to the New World, it was through his efforts and encouragement that the colony in New England was successfully established. He was initially motivated by a concern for English fishermen who usually sailed from the nearby port of Weymouth to American waters. How could they receive religious instruction during the nine- or ten-month period when they were away? With a resident minister and colony, the problem would be solved.

There were several unsuccessful expeditions under the auspices of the Dorchester Company, but Reverend White persevered. He raised money and ultimately procured the charter that was to be the start of the Commonwealth of Massachusetts. In 1629, with the backing of a Charter and the further support of a shipload of three hundred emigrants, the success of the new colony seemed secure. The colonists landed in an area which they named, naturally enough, "Dorchester" to honor their revered friend. A plaque in the First Parish Church of Dorchester, Massachusetts, reads: "Dorchester Named from the Town of Dorchester in Dorset England." The Church also has a tablet on either side of the doorway paying further tribute to Reverend John White.

Thomas Hardy has probably done more to bring visitors to Dorset than any Chamber of Commerce could hope to accomplish. The area of scenic beauty surrounding Dorchester has been immortalized in his works. There are panoramic views from Blagdon Hill where there is also a monument to the memory of Admiral Hardy, Nelson's Flag-Captain at Trafalgar. Nelson died in his arms, addressing his last words to this kinsman of the novelist.

But Thomas Hardy's inadvertent advertisements are everywhere.

Hangman's Cottage, believed to be the actual residence of the public hangman, with its pretty thatched roof, has a charm which belies its function. It is used in his story, "*The Withered Arm,*" and is a very popular tourist attraction, as evidenced by the clicking of cameras.

Abbotsbury, nine miles to the southwest, was founded as a Benedictine Abbey. It still has a well-preserved fifteenth-century Tithe Barn, mentioned in *Far from the Madding Crowd*. Abbotsbury also has Tropical Gardens with a fine collection of exotic trees. But most unusual is the Swannery, the only one in England. Owned and run by Lord Ilchester, it dates to the thirteenth century when it was established by the monks of Abbotsbury. The swans are marked on the left foot with Lord Ilchester's symbol two days after hatching. (Unmarked swans revert to the property of the Crown.)

The Bere Regis Church, eleven miles from Dorchester, has the Turberville window. (Yes, *Tess of the D'Urbervilles*.)

It is hardly possible to cover the settings in which Hardy's stories are based. Just as his memorializations are everywhere, so Dorchester has memorials to him. One statue, at the top of High West Street, is a life-size representation of the pensive poet resting with hat on crossed knees. Another Hardy Memorial statue, at the cottage in Higher Bockhampton where he was born, is the gift of American admirers.

Hardy lies buried in Westminster Abbey, but his heart is in Stinsford, in the "Mellstock" of his novels; there, just a mile and a half from Dorchester, it lies buried under the great yew tree in the churchyard.

The Museum may have the finest tribute of all to the literary giant of Dorset. The Thomas Hardy Memorial Room is a recreation of his study in the house he designed for himself at Max Gate. The room includes such memorabilia as his pens and copybook and original manuscript of *The Mayor of Casterbridge*. A roller calendar on his desk is set with the date of his original meeting with his first wife Emma—March 7, 1870. So it was set after she died and so it remained even when he married again.

Hardy's love of Dorset extended to archeology. In a paper entitled *Some Romano-British Relics found at Max Gate* and read in 1844, always the accurate observer, he recorded some remains found at Max Gate in Fordington Field and called for the reconstructing of bits of evidence of Roman life into a whole, much as has been done at Pompeii. He ponders what Romano-British life was like and asks probing questions: "What social character had the streets, what were the customary noises . . . Did they ever form a busy throng such as we now see on a market day? . . ." He is searching for life among the dead and dry jars, bowls, bottles, urns, and graves just as he created life and belonging in the pages of his books.

Thomas Hardy's Cottage in Higher Bockhampton

It is much easier, and alas disheartening, to assess life in today's Dorchester, where the customary sounds are traffic noises and even the shouting of voices necessarily raised to overcome the din of vehicles.

Although Dorchester is in a predominantly agricultural area, it does nevertheless have an assortment of inconspicuous industries. A printing industry, farm machinery factories, and leatherworks are hidden in the landscape. But the Dorchester Brewery is the largest and has been brewing beer in the town since the seventeenth century. Curiously, Dorchester ale has been famous since Tudor times. Hardy pays tribute to it (in *The Trumpet-Major*) when he says that "it was the most beautiful colour that the eye of an artist in beer could desire; full in body, yet brisk as a volcano; piquant, yet without a twang; luminous as an autumn sunset; free from streakiness of taste; but, finally, rather heady." How charming it would be to partake of the local brew in the smallest inn in the country—the Smith's Arms in Godmanstone, five miles north of Dorchester, which claims to be the smallest fully-licensed house in England.

But the scene in the center of town imparts no feeling of ancient charm, at least not superficially. It suggests rather that Hardy's description of the city is hardly accurate, that it is at best an exaggeration. The dominant feeling is that of a busy, commercial, trafficked center. Instead of Roman appearance, it has roaming crowds of shoppers. Instead of heading for an ancient forum, they throng to a modern shopping arcade. The word "antique" would seem to be relegated to shops which sport that epithet but which disappointingly purvey twentieth-century relics. And all "feeling" of the past would seem to be relegated to the Museum.

Nevertheless, things could be worse—much worse. The gift shops do *not* sell plastic replicas of the Hardy statue or T-shirts with the poet's picture. And the weekly markets *do* sell such delightful local products as Dorset cheese and Dorset butter. Moreover, the town is not only a convenient center for innumerable not-to-be-missed places within easy hiking or driving distance, but it can also be a pleasant town which offers escape from the bustle in its tree-lined avenues and its river bank, within easy walking distance from the center. Its active character leaves one with the final impression that Dorchester is by no means dormant.

Falmouth

Falmouth is a lovely seaport town with a climate so mild that oranges and bananas grow, palm trees line some streets, and tropical plants thrive in public gardens. The scene suggests a Mediterranean seaport town.

But Falmouth is a Cornish seaport town located on the English Channel, where its strategic importance has been appreciated through history. Sir Walter Raleigh called attention to the possibilities of the Fal estuary as an important deep water harbor. Earlier, in the 1540's, Henry VIII had built Pendennis Castle as part of his scheme for protecting England from possible attack by his Roman Catholic enemies. Built of Cornish granite, the defensive castle stands at the entrance of the Fal, guarding, together with its twin castle at St. Mawes on the other side of the river, the inland towns. These are perhaps the best preserved Tudor castles in the land—with apartments, huge fireplaces, spy holes, circular central towers, and angled bastions.

Although its history as a trading port may be quite ancient, the town of Falmouth itself goes back merely to the seventeenth century. Prior to that time, the site contained the small fishing hamlet known as Smithwick, or more popularly, Penny-come-quick (Actually, "Pen-y-cum-cuic" meant "head of the creek.") Also in the district was Arwenack, the major house of the Killigrews. The Killigrew family—gentlemen, pirates, and privateers—are credited as the founders of Falmouth. They started the building of the town in the 1620's, and Sir Peter Killigrew continued to foster its development after the Restoration in 1660. He secured a Charter from Charles II and gave the new and descriptive name of Falmouth to this little place. With its superb situation and nearly ten square miles of sheltered water, Falmouth soon outstripped other rival Cornish ports.

The selection of Falmouth as a Mail Packet Station in 1688 insured the prosperity of the town for the next century and a half. Falmouth became the western packet headquarters because of its proximity to the Continent and because of its good harbor. Sailing ships could enter and leave quickly, carrying mail to Spain and Portugal, to the West Indies and the Americas. The packet boats were privately owned and hired out to the Post Office. From this Post Office Packet Service came much of the town's wealth, still in evidence. For example, Captain John Bull who carried mail during the Napoleonic Wars on the famous ship, the Duke of Marlborough, built a mansion at Swanpool which he named after that ship. The Customs House on the quay dates from those times too.

Pendennis Castle

The contemporary Poet Laureate, Robert Southey, wrote in 1802 a vivid account of Falmouth life in its prosperous heyday:

> . . . Everybody is in a hurry here; either they are going off in Packets, and are hastening their preparations to embark; or they have just arrived, and are impatient to be on the road homeward. Every now and then a carriage rattles up to the door with a rapidity which makes the very house shake. The man who cleans the boots is running in one direction, the barber with his powder-bag in another; here goes the barber's boy with his hot water and razors; there comes the clean linen with the washerwoman; and the hall is full of porters and sailors bringing in luggage, or bearing it away; now you hear a horn blow because the post is coming in, and in the middle of the night you are awakened by another because it is going out. Nothing is done in England without a noise, and yet noise is the only thing they forget in the bill!

48

Falmouth lost the Packet Service (and perhaps the noise) in 1852 with the coming of the railway. Nevertheless, because of its continued use as a port, it did not suffer a serious decline. More important, its possibilities as a seaside resort were developed, and it became a vital ship repair base with huge dry docks. It was used in the Second World War, in June 1944, as a base for the dispatching of ships, armaments, and troops for the D-Day invasion.

Falmouth is an active commercial and industrial town but with enough antiquities and memories to conjure up an image of the past. The waterfront is still the heart of Falmouth. Even the main shopping street curves to follow the shore line and is connected to quays by alleys called "opes." Old combines with new. A fragment of the Killigrew mansion remains as part of a modern house on the sea front—a reminder of the ambitious beginnings of a town still thriving in a state of warm, friendly, and beautiful youth, a town which faces the sea as if to pay tribute to the source of its vitality.

Falmouth is as "young" as some American cities, having recently celebrated its tercentenary. In 1961, just three hundred years after receiving a Charter from Charles II, Falmouth was granted a Coat of Arms which includes in its heraldic design a Packet Boat in full sail at its crest. At its base is water which represents the Fal and the sea as well as a most appropriate motto, "Remember."

Framlingham

Compared with its counterpart in England, Framingham in Massachusetts has lost its "l"—and more. Although early colonial records, including the Diary of Cotton Mather, spell the American Framingham with the "l," it began to be common practice some three hundred years ago to omit the letter in writing. In speech, the letter is frequently unsounded, even today.

The approach to Framingham in New England is via a busy highway and major shopping centers. The visitor to Framlingham in old England is confronted with the sight of a noble ruin—a huge castle which rises high up on a mound used and built by the Saxons as fortification some twelve centuries ago in "the village of Framela's people."

The castle is the focal point of Framlingham, but Framingham history focuses on one man—Nicholas Danforth. A Churchwarden in the reign of King Charles I and an early emigrant to the New World, this seventeenth-century Framlingham yeoman owned seventy acres of land and lived in a timber-framed house of two floors believed to have been built no later than the reign of Queen Elizabeth I. He was probably born in that house, now called New Street Farm and now a private residence located about a mile and a half from the town center on the road to Saxtead.

Six years after his wife died, Nicholas Danforth left for America with six of his seven children. That was in the year 1635, just fifteen years after the Mayflower had sailed. He died in Cambridge, Massachusetts, in 1638, aged about 48, but left behind a progeny of notables said to be represented in every state of the United States.

His eldest son Thomas held several political and civic offices including Treasurer of Harvard University, Deputy Governor, and Associate Judge of Superior Court. His second son, Rev. Samuel Danforth, was one of the first five fellows of Harvard. One descendant, Josiah Quincy, became president of Harvard University. Another descendant, James Abram Garfield, became president of the United States.

It was the son of the founder of this noble family who founded the American town of Framingham. Thomas Danforth owned the plantation known originally as Danforth's Farms before it was named for the original and beloved home of its first inhabitants from the charming market town in Suffolk.

In that market town today, the castle is the main attraction. The first castle on the site is believed to have been built by the Saxon kings of East

50

Anglia, the last of whom was Saint Edmund. He was captured by Danish invaders and died at their hands in 870, a Christian martyr. Framlingham became the seat of the Earls and Dukes of Norfolk, and the Second Earl of Norfolk, Roger le Bigod built the castle as seen today, circa 1190. This powerful nobleman was present at the coronations of King Richard I, King Richard II, and King John. It is he who appears as "Lord Bigot" in Shakespeare's *King John*.

Framlingham Castle

The medieval walls of Framlingham Castle are over forty feet high and in places eight feet thick, with foundations that go thirty feet below ground. It is surrounded by double moat, now dry of course, with a bowling green between the inner and outer moats. The ancient game of bowls is believed to have been played here some six hundred years ago.

Perhaps the most famous historic event that took place in the castle occurred in the summer of 1553 when Princess Mary withdrew to the Duke of Norfolk's Castle of Framlingham after the death of King Edward VI. With the help of supporters, she was here proclaimed Queen of England.

Framlingham has a fifteenth-century church with a nearly one-hundred-foot-high tower. The chancel of the Church of St. Michael is an unusual architectural feature because of its disproportionate size. As if giving way to Middle Ages spread, it is wider than the nave. It is also full of monuments and history and monumental history.

Chief among the monuments is that of Henry Howard, known in literature as the poet Earl of Surrey. Surrey, son and heir of the third Duke of Norfolk, was convicted on a charge of high treason and beheaded on Tower Hill. He lies resplendent alongside his wife, with two sons kneeling at their feet and three daughters at the head of the alabaster tomb. He wears rich red robes trimmed with white ermine and gold clasp. Sadly, his coronet rests by his pillow to signify that he was beheaded.

Another of the six effigy tombs in the chancel is that of Thomas Howard, third Duke of Norfolk (1473-1554). He was Surrey's father and the uncle of Queen Anne Boleyn and Queen Catherine Howard. Above his tomb, in the chancel wall, is the Flodden helm which he wore at the Battle of Flodden in 1513. The words on the collar of his effigy, "By the Grace of God I am what I am" refer to his fortuitous escape with head intact when Henry VIII conveniently died on the day preceding the scheduled execution. In one of those ironic twists of history, if Henry VIII had had the grace or judgment to die one day sooner, the Duke's son, the poet Surrey, would have avoided his untimely death as well.

Relatively recent history of the town includes the new Framlingham College which was founded as the Suffolk county memorial to Prince Albert. Its facts and features include an eight-foot high bronze statue of the Prince Consort, an enrollment of over four hundred boys, over thirty-five acres of playing fields, and an impressive site on high ground with views of Framlingham Castle and Church. Opened in 1865 by Queen Victoria, this "new" bit of Framlingham history has already celebrated its centenary.

The small and appealing town is filled with a sense of history, peace, and beauty. In the center, Market Hill is delightful. The Crown Hotel dates in part from the sixteenth century. Its massive open timbers of old English domestic architecture and eighteenth-century staircase with carved balustrade are admirable.

Also in Market Hill is the former Guildhall, now called London House, with an interesting oak-paneled room. It has been a drapery store ever since it was rebuilt by Simon Pulham around 1584.

New Road offers a mixture. Sir Robert Hitcham's Almshouses, a picturesque group of six houses for men and six for women was built in 1654 from stones of buildings razed inside the castle walls. Also in New Road are a cinema, a factory, and good views of castle and church.

The charming country town with good shops, hotels, and pubs offers a retreat just 88 miles from London to a romantic vision summed up by the poet James Bird (1788-1839) in his poem "Framlingham":

> . . . fair castled Town,
> Rare spot of beauty, grandeur, and renown,
> Seat of Anglican kings!

52

Gloucester

That Gloucester is located on water seems natural enough and not surprising to anyone who knows and loves Gloucester in Massachusetts. Gloucester, England, is also located on the water. But it is situated on a river, the Severn, which broadens out, before flowing into the Bristol Channel, to give the appearance of an inland sea. Furthermore, in England, rather than pounding waves against dignified masses of rocks, rather than sandy stretches of beach, one is more likely to witness an unfamiliar and awesome phenomenon known as the Severn Bore. This natural phenomenon occurs on other estuaries, but not with such spectacular results. Simply, the Bore is a tide which meets the ebbing water and becomes a wave. The tidal waters of the river become more and more constricted as the river bed narrows above Sharpness (some thirty miles from Gloucester by river). Then, as the tidal waters approach Gloucester, they become a high wall of water, stretching across the width of the river and driving forward at a speed of about sixteen miles an hour. It may reach a height of nine or ten feet and take the form of a biblical spectacle. Defoe describes the Bore ". . . rolling forward like a mighty wave: so that the stern of a vessel shall in a sudden be lifted up six or seven feet upon the water. . . ." The Bore phenomenon, which occurs each month at the full moon, may be of a lesser degree. The local press announces favorable conditions for viewing.

As if that were not sufficiently breathtaking, the visitor approaching from the east, from London, goes through some of the most beautiful, picturesque countryside to be found anywhere. The famed region of hilly country known as the Cotswolds offers sweeping landscapes with gently rolling hills which unroll and reveal hidden villages. Vistas are greatly enhanced by the characteristic building material used for houses, cottages, and churches as well as for the stone walling which separates the fields. If you can get through this photographer's paradise without being permanently entranced by the Saxon or Norman churches, quaint bridges, typical Cotswold architecture, or Roman remains, you come to the City of Gloucester.

The city is of great antiquity and carries a name over two thousand years old. Before Roman times, its name was "Caer Glow." *Caer* is the British for an enclosure or town, and *Glowe* is generally agreed to mean "fair." After the Roman invasion, it was given the Latinized form of "Glevum." It reverted, in Saxon times, to something like its original form. "Glow-caestre," "Glewan-cester" and "Glew-ceastre" are Saxon versions of Glevum Town, Fair City.

53

Gloucester Port

The great attraction of this cathedral town is, not surprisingly, its cathedral. Formerly the abbey church, the Norman influence can still be seen even though the earlier church was largely destroyed by fire in 1122 and rebuilt. The present building resulted from the slow rebuilding which took place over the fourteenth and fifteenth centuries.

The great east window, one of the largest medieval stained-glass windows in the country, is undoubtedly the greatest glory of the cathedral. Its forty-nine figures, with central theme of the Coronation of the Virgin, allows light through its translucent tints, giving the east end of the choir, which it nearly fills, the loveliest effect. It may even be thought of as one of the first war memorials, for it was installed in 1350 by Lord Bradeston, Governor of Gloucester Castle, in memory of his good friend, and other knights, killed in battle with the French in 1346. One interesting memorial effigy is to Jenner—that local doctor who is credited with the demise of the smallpox scourge.

Among the great events which have taken place in the Gloucester Abbey

54

was the order by William the Conqueror in 1086 to compile the Domesday Book, that written record of all English property. There was also the hasty coronation, upon the sudden death of King John in 1216, of his eldest son Henry. Henry III, a youth of nine, was made to pledge at his coronation to govern according to Magna Carta, a pledge he broke, as did his father earlier.

Parliament met in Gloucester on a number of occasions including the year 1378 when young King Richard II was ten years old, and his uncle, John of Gaunt, manipulated a politically expedient meeting away from Westminster, where he was extremely unpopular. Among the distinguished visitors are Henry VIII who arrived in 1535 with his Queen, Anne Boleyn. James II slept here too, on a visit which took place in 1687.

Gloucester was declared a Port City by the charter granted in 1580 by Elizabeth I. Its excellent facilities for water transport, as well as later rail, road, and air transport, have insured that Gloucester would remain an industrial center. Even before the Conquest, it was active with the casting of iron as its chief industry. A bell foundry, dating from about 1270, existed for nearly six hundred years. For a long time, the city did a large trade in pins, introduced by John Tylsley in 1626. Before that time thorns were scraped, trimmed, dried, and used for pins. All pin manufacturing seems now to have moved to Birmingham, and while other industries have moved out, newer ones have moved in. Gloucester is today a center for such manufactures as aviation equipment, man-made fibers, farm equipment, and the production of ice cream.

The modern city, predictably, bustles with shopping centers, cattle market, schools and libraries, parks, hospitals, museums and art gallery. In the City Museum are archeological finds from prehistoric, Roman, and medieval times, excavated from underneath the modern city.

The Beautiful Port, Champlain named the American city—a name that could apply as well to the English city. How appropriate, therefore, that the American settlers renamed their city in remembrance of the one in England from which they had emigrated.

Groton

A road map of East Anglia shows a complex of red, green, and yellow lines which indicate the primary and secondary roads leading from London through some of the most beautiful scenery of Suffolk. But a road that is merely lined in and without color leads to the tiny, colorful village of Groton, sixty-three miles northeast of London. Actually, Groton is a parish, not even a village, located within a cluster of surrounding hamlets.

Although the history of Groton goes back to before Domesday Book, that survey ordered by William the Conqueror in 1086, it is relatively recent history that singles out Groton and locates it on the American Heritage Trail. Groton is a historical shrine, for it was the home of John Winthrop, whose influence in the early history of New England is immeasurable.

The Church of St. Bartholomew, which hides in quiet countryside, dominates. A prominent sign before the entrance announces:

> John Winthrop. Leader of the Puritan Emigration to New England in 1630 Founder of Boston and First Governor of Massachusetts U.S.A. was Patron of this Church and Lord of the Manor 1618-1630.

Already, at the time of the Norman Conquest, the county of Suffolk was given the nickname of *Seelig* (meaning "Holy") for its great number of parish churches. Some four hundred existed at the time of Domesday, and nearly one hundred more were added by mid-thirteenth century. Because England's wealth came largely from wool, Suffolk, an important wool-weaving center, was able to procure the best craftsmanship for its numerous churches. So it is not surprising that the Groton Parish Church, St. Bartholomew's, with its nave and clerestory, chancel and aisles, and its thirteenth-century Early English tower is an impressive building.

All around are memorials and tombs of John Winthrop and his family. The large stained-glass east window of 1875 was erected to the memory of John Winthrop. His father and grandfather are buried in the chancel. Also buried in the chancel are John Winthrop's first two wives and the infant daughter of the latter. His third wife died in Boston in 1647, and he married for the fourth time in 1648. He himself died in 1649 and is buried in the grounds of King's Chapel in Boston.

An interesting entry in the Church Register records the marriage in 1622 of Lucy Winthrop, sister of John Winthrop, to Emanuel Downing, later a resident of New England. Their son, Sir George Downing, one of the first graduates of Harvard College in 1642, has had the famous Downing Street of London named after him.

56

Groton Parish Church

The windows of the organ chamber in the north aisle contain shields of the Winthrop family and of Massachusetts, with an Indian in gold against a blue background.

Of the ancient Manor of Groton, nothing remains but the mulberry tree. It stands in what was once Winthrop's garden. Mulberry trees must be signs of greatness, for one of equal renown stands in the court of Christ's College, Cambridge—Milton's mulberry tree.

The Manor of Groton belonged to the Abbey of Bury St. Edmunds in the eleventh century. At the Dissolution of the Monasteries by Henry VIII, Adam Winthrop was allowed to purchase the Manor in 1544. He was the first Lord of the Manor and Patron of the Church, a position later inherited by his grandson. John Winthrop, born in 1588 in the adjoining village of Edwardstone, sold his interest to follow up on new interests in the New World.

Several shiploads of Suffolk families, including many from the Groton district, sailed with John Winthrop in 1630 when he went out on the *Arabella* to the colony of Massachusetts. He proved to be an intelligent and able leader who earned for himself the accolade, "The Father of New England."

The governor's son, Deane Winthrop, gave the name of his native place of Groton in England to the Groton in Massachusetts, which was incorporated in 1655.

The origin of the name Groton is derived from the Anglo-Saxon *Grotan*, meaning coarsely ground oats, as in the word *groats*. It has been suggested that the tract of land which overlooks the valley of the River Box was gravelly or gritty. If the Old English word *Grot* means a particle, it also appropriately names a grain of sand on the map.

But it must be true that great groats from little gravels grow, for the sailing from the Groton district in 1630 transplanted not only names of old Suffolk homes and distinguished men and women, but it established a strong and everlasting Anglo-American bond.

Haverhill

The history of modern Haverhill, on the Essex-Suffolk border in England, begins in the eighth century with an Anglo-Saxon settlement on the western edge of the present town. It was a trading community that profited from its position as a half-way stage between Cambridge and Sudbury. The trade probably specialized in oats, as "Haver" means oats.

Haverhill's development in the Middle Ages is typical of an East Anglian market town. It is listed in the Domesday Survey of 1086, and by the middle of the thirteenth century, all roads entering Haverhill passed through the market place for easy collection of tolls. The town's wealth was based on the weekly market and important annual fairs. The town thrived, and a new church was built in the thirteenth century.

Wool and wealth came to Haverhill in the fourteenth century. The town rebuilt and enlarged the parish church and established handsome guild and civic buildings. Prosperity continued into the seventeenth century with the arrival of new weaving techniques brought by Flemish refugees. Sales of "Haverhill" cloth are recorded in London. Gurteen, a weaver from nearby Clare, moved to Haverhill and established the family industry which is still a vital part of the town's economy.

Its counterpart on the banks of the Merrimac River in Massachusetts was settled in about 1640 by the Reverend John Ward and named Haverhill for his home in England. Dr. Mather writes of this eminent worthy of New England and states that "his grandfather was that John Ward the worthy minister of Haverhill, and his father was that Nathanial Ward, whose wit made him known to more Englands than one."

Alas, little remains of the homestead he left. A fire of 1665 destroyed the town. Its church was greatly damaged, its guild and civic buildings were utterly demolished, and the population was reduced to unemployment and poverty. The town recovered slowly during the eighteenth century. It was the middle of the nineteenth century however, with the coming of the Industrial Revolution and the railroads, that was a period of development.

Consequently, most of present-day Haverhill is a Victorian factory town with rows of dreary brick houses. Apart from Weaver's Row with its twelve fine weaver's houses, there is little of interest for the tourist. A major landmark is the factory of D. Gurteen & Son. On the edge of town, a sign suggests Victorian delicacy by pointing to the "Civic Amenity"—town dump.

Haverhill, a small town fifty-five miles northeast of London, offers views of the hills and dreams of the past.

Ipswich

Ipswich was Gipswich. It was the dwelling of Gipi, the leader of those seafaring Anglo-Saxons who took full advantage of the position at the head of the River Orwell estuary where the River Gipping joins it. The settlement became a flourishing trade community by the ninth century and was one of the most prosperous of English towns at the time of the Norman conquest.

In the year 1200, King John granted the town its first Charter, and the seal of the town further corroborates the importance of trading; it depicts a primitive ship, the earliest known example of the type of sailing vessel with a fixed rudder, the type that could easily ply its way up the river along Ipswich quays.

Trading has continued to play a role in the fortunes of the town. In the thirteenth and fourteenth centuries much of the local wool, considered the finest in Europe, was shipped to Flanders to be made into cloth. In the next two centuries, wool was made into cloth in England and then shipped. Only when the industry moved to the west and north from East Anglia, in the seventeenth and eighteenth centuries, did the town decline. But with the opening up of railway communication and with harbor improvements, industry grew and Ipswich revived.

The extensive woolen cloth trade of the Middle Ages has been supplanted by a wide range of all sorts of cargo. Today, Ipswich manufactures and exports such items as farm machinery, construction equipment, heating systems, garments, baked goods, and beer. And Ipswich remains one of the busiest and most important ports of the east coast.

One variation of a maritime theme links Ipswich with America. In New England, the region known as Agawam was settled by John Winthrop, Jr., son of the Governor. He purchased land from the Indians for twenty pounds and led a group of settlers to the site in 1633. Captain John Smith had landed in Agawam in 1614 and wrote of it that it would make "an excellent habitation, being a good and safe harbor."

Indeed, the land was bountiful, and Pastor Higginson of Salem records that "our turnips, parsnips and carrots are here both bigger and sweeter than is ordinary to be found in England." And perhaps many would maintain that he was carried away on an air of enthusiasm when he recorded that "a sup of New England aire is better than a whole draught of English ale."

In any case, the settlement took root and thrived, and on August 4, 1634, the Court decreed that Agawam be called Ipswich after Ipswich in England "in acknowledgement of the great honor and kindness done to our people who took shipping there." Moreover, the name honored the son of John Ward of Ipswich, England, the Reverend Nathaniel Ward. This uncompromising Puritan sought refuge in the New World. There he landed in 1634 and spent his first winter in Ipswich. (His own son, John Ward, was instrumental in naming the nearby town of Haverhill).

Any similarity between the two Ipswiches today centers on access and position in regard to the sea. Otherwise, the characteristic New England town is similar to its mother town in name only. What is Ipswich in Suffolk like today?

The Port of Ipswich, the biggest port between the Humber and the Thames, handles millions of tons of cargo each year. There is a Wet Dock which can accommodate ships up to 275 feet long and Cliff Quay which can accommodate ships at any state of the tide. The busy port is continuously developing, and new facilities and changes are constantly taking place.

Old merchants' houses survive near the docks. The Neptune Inn in Fore Street, now a private residence and antique shop, was a dwelling even earlier than the date of 1639 which appears on its front. Nearby is Isaac Lord's house with an inner courtyard leading to a warehouse on the quayside. The Eldred House once stood in this district, but relics of the house are now in Christchurch Mansion Museum. Thomas Eldred was an adventurer who sailed through the Straits of Magellan with Thomas Cavendish and was one of fifty men to survive that rough second voyage made by Cavendish around the world.

Another merchant of fame was John Chaucer, a vintner who took his name from the *chausses* which vintners carried as deck cargo on their wine ships. The name was immortalized by his son Geoffrey Chaucer, the great English poet. Although Geoffrey Chaucer was a Londoner and a courtier, he understood the vintries of Ipswich and the quayside in the Port of Orwell, as expressed in the Prologue to the *Canterbury Tales* by his description of the pompous Merchant with a forked beard:

> He wolde the see were kept for anythyng
> Bitwixe Middelburgh and Orewelle.

From the wealthy merchants and trade of the Middle Ages came the numerous medieval churches which are sprinkled through the town. In modern times, however, the churches are rapidly becoming redundant.

One closed church is St. Mary at the Quay, with a fine hammerbeam roof and several important memorial brasses (removed to Christchurch Mansion Museum) including the famous Pounder brass engraved in 1525 by a Flemish artist. The merchant Thomas Pounder is shown wearing rich fur-trimmed gown, with his wife beside him, while two sons and six daughters kneel at their feet. The town's great merchant and benefactor Henry Tooley and his wife Alice were buried here as well, and a wall brass of 1551 depicts them kneeling in prayer with their children. Naturally, this merchant family derived its riches from the trade of the port. Tooley dealt in fishing industry, importing of wines, and in canvas and fabric including a new type of colored cloth called a "medley."

Also disused is the Church of St. Clement, close to the wharves and cranes of the docks and hemmed in by commercial buildings. Long known as the Sailors' Church, it was built in the fourteenth century when the port was at a peak of prosperity and served sailors and people who worked on the docks. Inside is the tomb of Thomas Eldred and a stone monument to Chevalier Cobbold. The Cobbold family is an important name in Ipswich, known as brewers and appreciated by imbibers. The Church has a fifteenth-century nave with an extremely fine example of clerestory and suggests medieval beauty in a seaside corner of Ipswich.

But the heart of Ipswich has largely lost its seafaring atmosphere. Ipswich presents itself as a bustling, partly industrialized town, choked with traffic in its center around the Buttermarket, the street which once included stalls for the sale of dairy products and poultry as well as for butter. The spires and towers of old churches are dominated by new building blocks, but the medieval pattern of the narrow, congested streets contains interesting old buildings everywhere.

Ipswich is proud of its ancient house in the Buttermarket called the Ancient House. It is a gorgeous example of an ornate plaster decoration known as "pargeting." The sculptured symbols below four oriel windows represent the continents—America, Asia, Africa, and Europe. Australia was unknown when the house was built in 1567. For two hundred years it was the home of the Sparrowe family, and it is said that that family, ardent Royalists, sheltered and hid King Charles II in a secret room. Indeed, the interior remains fit for a king. In the rooms are such features as oak-paneled walls, a carved plaster ceiling, and a Tudor fireplace. The building now functions as the very fine Ancient House Bookshop.

St. Stephens, with a lovely west tower overlooking the Ancient House is disused, as is the nearby St. Lawrence.

Just as the Buttermarket is not restricted to the sale of butter, so Cornhill is no longer the place where corn is sold. Rather, public buildings are located in this wide space in the center of town known as Cornhill. In the square is the Italian-style Town Hall, built in 1868 with domed tower and clock with four faces. The Corn Exchange adjoins the Town Hall. Next to it is the unusually ornate Post Office.

62

The Ancient House

Also in the town center, on a busy corner, is the White Horse Inn, an old coaching inn of Dickensian fame where Mr. Pickwick lost his way in the corridor and had an interesting encounter with a "middle-aged lady, in yellow curl-papers." The white horse can still be seen over the doorway, unkindly described by Dickens as "some rampacious animal with flowing mane and tail, distantly resembling an insane cart-horse." Unlike Dickens,

Americans thought enough of this coaching inn to build a full-scale replica of it at their World's Fair in Chicago.

St. Mary-Le-Tower is so named because it stood near a tower of the old town walls, along the line of the present road, Tower Ramparts. This principal parish church was largely rebuilt in the 1860's, and its present appearance may be attributed to Victorian tastes. Still, there is a fifteenth-century font, an oak pulpit of about 1700, and medieval misericords in the chancel. Parish record books of the seventeenth and eighteenth centuries contain minutes which suggest that meetings may have been too long, for they "ordered that this Meeting be adjourned to the White Horse Tavern."

St. Margaret's is more spectacular. Set against the background of Christchurch Park, it has a fifteenth-century double-hammerbeam roof, a beautiful clerestory, and attractive decorations all over. A font is carved with eight angels, one of which holds a scroll with the inscription, "Sal et Saliva," indicating the use of salt and spittle in an ancient baptism ceremony.

Just north of St. Margaret's Church, in the spacious Christchurch Park, originally outside the old town walls, is Christchurch Mansion, a fine Tudor structure. Edmund Withipoll, a London merchant, purchased the property of the Augustinian Priory of 1177 which had been suppressed in 1537 and began the building in 1548 of a typical E-plan red brick Tudor mansion. Among its features are rooms with Tudor paneling, the hall with minstrel's gallery, and kitchen with great fireplace equipped for work. Queen Elizabeth (who slept in more places than George Washington) is supposed to have slept in this house when she visited Ipswich in 1561 and again in 1565. It is now filled with mementos of Ipswich history and maintained as a museum and art gallery. Its collection of paintings by the masters features works of those local artists, Constable and Gainsborough. Gainsborough started his career in Ipswich, where he lived for fifteen years following his marriage at the age of eighteen to an Ipswich girl.

Also in this period, an unknown actor, greatly encouraged by enthusiastic Ipswich audiences, went in 1741 to London under his real name of David Garrick where he made an immediate and sensational success.

Cardinal Wolsey, who may be the most distinguished person associated with Ipswich, was born here in 1471. He had already founded his college at Oxford (Christ Church) when he began the building in 1528 of what was planned as a grand school in Ipswich, intended to outdo Eton or for that matter anything at Oxford or Cambridge. But the grandiose plans for his native town were aborted and the building never completed. When Wolsey fell from power, his college fell too. Completely destroyed, only the simple red brick Tudor gateway with the arms of Henry VIII above the arch

64

Tudor Gateway of Wolsey's College

survives just alongside St. Peter's. Thus is the double fall described to Queen Katherine in Shakespeare's *King Henry the Eighth:*

> Ever witness for him
> Those twins of learning that he rais'd in you,
> Ipswich, and Oxford, one of which fell with him!
> Unwilling to outlive the good that did it.

With so many relics of history, with the scale and quality of its many historic and ancient buildings, with a situation in unspoiled Suffolk countryside about 68 miles northeast of London, it is no wonder that the words are still applicable with which Daniel Defoe described Ipswich over 250 years ago as "one of the most agreeable places in England."

65

King's Lynn

It is unlikely that a traveler would pass through isolated Norfolk by mere chance. Norfolk is an out-of-the-way county, characterized as flat (some would say "dull"), located in the area known as East Anglia, some one hundred miles north of London. So the visitor would normally have a reason, perhaps a business reason, for going to the port of King's Lynn. But no excuse is needed for enjoying the delights of a town which exudes charm and character and takes the visitor back to Olde England.

King's Lynn, known as just plain Lynn, has an ancient and engaging character that can be explained on the basis of geography. Located on the River Great Ouse, near the Wash, it has always been an important outlet to the sea, and its wealth has always been rooted in trade. In the Middle Ages, Lynn was a primary port of England; it vied with Boston (on the other side of the Wash) for the export of riches from the English interior, particularly wool. And it continues to be an important port.

Lynn, with medieval remnants and reminders of history and tradition, is one of the most romantic towns in all of England. Starting with the Guildhall of the Holy Trinity, the visitor may see art and myth and history romanticized. The building itself, with an exterior chequer-board pattern of flint and stone, dates from 1421. Inside, is a spacious Stone Hall with an impressive Perpendicular window and a beautiful Assembly Room. The Trinity Guildhall houses many of the treasures of Lynn including the King John Sword and the well-known King John Cup. King John visited Lynn on several occasions and is credited with having presented his own sword to the town in 1204. But the story that the Cup was presented on the occasion of another of the King's visits, when he lost his valuable baggage in the Wash, does not withstand the test of historical accuracy. Nevertheless, the gilded and enamelled Cup with hunting and hawking scenes is an important and beautiful treasure.

If the Trinity Guildhall can be recognized by its chequered front, St. George's Guildhall is distinguished for its chequered history, having served as a corn exchange, theatre, and warehouse. It was the theatre in Elizabethan times. Here, Shakespeare's company is known to have played. Indeed it is likely that Shakespeare himself appeared on stage. Appropriately, it has been restored for use again as a theatre and is the center for the annual King's Lynn Festival of Music and the Arts. This marvellous festival, which has been taking place each summer since 1951, came about as an idea to help preserve the early fifteenth-century Guildhall.

66

Towards the end of July, the finest orchestras, conductors, singers, instrumentalists, and actors perform in this "mini-Edinburgh" of the Fens.

In Lynn, sea associations are strong and almost continuous. Along the quayside, in King Street, is a graceful Customs House, built in 1683, and designed by the local architect, Henry Bell. It is a square gem of two stories, surmounted by a lantern tower, and in a niche above the main entrance stands a statue of King Charles II.

Customs House

Along the ancient waterfront are some of the finest medieval merchants' combined houses and warehouses in the country. A fourteenth-century wealthy merchant's town house known as Hampton Court has now been restored for use as flats. There is the long Hanseatic Warehouse of 1428, which goes back to the river. And the medieval Clifton House gives a good view of the town from its Elizabethan brick watch tower of five stories.

The towers of St. Margaret's Church overlook the old warehouses. Portions of this fine church, such as the southwest tower, date to the twelfth century. A mythical account explains the name of the church. St. Margaret

67

is supposed to have slain an evil dragon. For that admirable deed, the pretty, lovable, pious Christian maiden won the unwanted love of Olybius, the Roman general. Naturally, she refused to marry him, and was, therefore, in the year 278, beheaded. Margaret, the tutelar Saint of Lynn, can be seen on the official seal, trampling the distorted body of the dragon while piercing his head with her cross. The Church is dedicated to her honor.

Among the features to be viewed inside are the Early English chancel with circular east window, elaborate reredos, fourteenth-century choir stalls with carved heads including those of Edward III and the Black Prince, and incomparable monumental brasses.

Norfolk has more memorial brasses than any other county, and the two largest brasses in England, both of Flemish workmanship, both nearly ten feet long, are located in St. Margaret's. The Peacock brass depicts Robert Braunche, who died in 1364, with his two wives. It is so named because on it is inscribed a scene which shows him giving a sumptuous banquet to King Edward III in 1349 at which a peacock is being served. The other brass, memorializing Adam de Walsokne and his wife, is dated 1349, the year of the great plague, and is embellished with a rustic scene depicting corn being taken to a windmill.

The market day tradition is strong in King's Lynn where there are two markets, one for Tuesday and the other for Saturday. The Tuesday Market, founded in the twelfth century, is a large open area of three acres which takes on an especially cheerful and colorful appearance once a week but retains its festive charm always. The dominant Duke's Head Hotel, also designed by Henry Bell, is one of the architecturally pleasing buildings in the square. One street, in the north-east corner, leads to St. Nicholas Chapel with more medieval memories.

Even the market scene suggests certain sea associations; the fresh fruits and vegetables displayed here serve as a further reminder of the produce from surrounding farmland which still keeps the harbor busy. In fact, the very farmland has been reclaimed from the sea. From earliest times, when the very first settlers began to inhabit the Fens, they not only depended on river or sea for their livelihood, but they also contended with the severe winter floods which were quite usual for the area. The Fens have since been drained and reclaimed for agricultural use. One unusual crop in this rich food-producing area is lavender. The large acreage of attractive color and aroma draws many visitors and not a few bees.

Associations with the sea continue to be strong in the still substantial fishing industry. Between the Alexandra and the Bentinck docks is the waterway known as the Fisher Fleet. Here the tiny fishing boats land with

68

their catches. Here local artists, photographers, and visitors gather to take in the local color and perhaps a few local samples. If you are ever going to try fresh cockles, Lynn is the place—on the docks, straight from the sea.

Although the Red Mount Chapel stands away from the water area in a park-like setting called the Walks, it too manages to be bound up with the sea. Indeed, it owes its very existence to the sea. This unique wayside oratory was built in 1485 for use by pilgrims. Anyone taking a medieval vacation, a pilgrimage, was likely to leave from Lynn, the port for the shrine at Walsingham. The small, exquisite chapel in the upper story of this red brick, octagonal building is built in the fashion of a cross and has a delicate, fan-vaulted ceiling, among the finest extant.

King's Lynn is a delight for wanderers with an eye to making new discoveries and finds (possibly even King John's lost treasure). In just a small area bordered by the waterfront, something of interest exists in every street and at every turning. The narrow streets and fine medieval buildings exude an old world character which remains to be felt all around and particularly along King Street, which leads from the Tuesday Market and changes its name to Queen Street after taking a slight bend.

For contrast to the romantic past, parallel to King Street is the realistic present in High Street a modern, bustling, shopping, walking street where one can buy new things (instead of discovering them) and, over a pot of tea, contemplate the changes wrought by time. For a much nastier shock back to reality, there is the heavily-trafficked John Kennedy Road.

Further afield, the variations are endless. For example, nearby are the royal estates at Sandringham. Or there is Walsingham, that famous pilgrimage spot since 1061. There is the tiny timeless village of Castle Rising, once a Norman fortress complete with castle, as its name implies, with a perfect Norman church. Along the North Norfolk coast are some of the sandiest, sunniest, loneliest beaches in England. And some forty miles from Lynn is Cambridge.

So persistent are associations with the sea, that the very name of the town itself hearkens back to it. The name *Lynn* derives from a Celtic word meaning "pool" or "lake" and is thus a modest description of a marshy area in the Norfolk fenland once covered by the sea and floods. The spelling *Lynn* did not come to be used until the seventeenth century. Earlier variants include *Len* or *Lenn*, and the Norman scribe in Domesday Book calls it *Lena* and *Lun*. During the Middle Ages, the town was known as Bishop's Lynn. But a 1537 charter of Henry VIII changed the name to Lynn Regis or King's Lynn, as it is officially known. The locals drop the formal "King's" and refer to their town in the familiar form, "Lynn."

And that was the name chosen for the Massachusetts counterpart to honor Rev. Samuel Whiting, who left his Church of St. Margaret in Lynn and embarked for the American wilderness just sixteen years after the Pilgrim Fathers set sail. There he worked for forty-three years, until his death in 1679. The American Lynn has long outgrown, commercially, its older and more humble namesake, the small and beautiful town of King's Lynn.

Laxton

The scenery of Nottinghamshire—Sherwood Forest and Robin Hood legends notwithstanding—is dotted with collieries and factories. The midst of the Midlands is modern, smoky, and industrial, sustaining any impression of an unattractive coal mining industry that may have been created in the novels of D. H. Lawrence. What a jolt it is, therefore, to find an ancient village, not only wholly argicultural, but with a system of farming that is over a thousand years old.

The village of Laxton, known in earlier times also as Lexington, is in the center of Nottinghamshire on the eastern edge of Sherwood Forest. Narrow roads connect it to adjacent farming communities, but two major highways on either side bypass it and leave this quiet segment of the county isolated. Thus, the chance tourist is not likely to find the way to Laxton and its intriguing past nor to realize that this ancient village is the ancestor of Lexington, Massachusetts.

What happens to names through the ages? Framlingham loses an *l* and Billericay loses a *y*. Maldon undergoes a spelling change. In England, Nottingham loses its initial *S* from the original Anglo-Saxon town of Snotingham. But Lexington loses a syllable and becomes Laxton. Largely disused by the early seventeenth century, the name "Lexington" is Saxon. The first part of the name refers to the original head of the community, and the *-ing* root refers to "the descendants or people of." It is the tun, or farm, of the people of Leaxa.

An entry in the Domesday Survey of 1086 refers to "Laxintune." Other documents refer to such a variety of names as Lexintun and Lexinton, Laxington and Lessington.

At the time of the Norman Conquest, Laxton was held by Tochi, son of Outi. But William the Conqueror granted it to Geoffrey Alselin, the great Norman baron. Other lords of the manor who succeeded him include Robert de Caux, builder of the castle; Robert and John de Lexington, judges and administrators; their brother Henry, bishop of Lincoln in 1253; Robert de Everingham, Adam de Everingham, and so on, to the present owner of the estate, the Minister of Agriculture.

Laxton is the only place left in England where the open field system of agriculture is still practiced, using land tenure methods unchanged since Saxon times. Each farmer changes his land year by year. Three great fields of about three hundred acres each—West Field, Mill Field, and South Field—are further divided into strips of about three and a quarter acres to be

Dovecote Inn

distributed among the tenants. Yearly, in rotation, wheat is planted in one field and crops in another, while the third lies fallow.

The system persisted as would have been natural under primitive conditions. A long narrow strip was most convenient for a plough drawn by a clumsy team of oxen—long to avoid having to make awkward turns more often than necessary, and narrow to limit the area to what could be ploughed in a day. Strips were scattered to insure more equal distribution of good land among the farmers.

The manorial court which administers the system still meets annually. It appoints a jury to inspect fields and to insure that customs of the manor are observed. After their inspection, after they have driven in any new boundary stakes and made necessary repairs, the jury members repair to the Dovecote Inn for a repast. Refreshments are paid for in part by proceeds from fines that have been collected by the court.

After the harvesting of crops, the fields are open for common grazing, and stretches of meadow at the ends of the furrows are auctioned off for the right to cut hay. The bidding is open to those who, in the words of the ancient rules, "have smoke up a chimney in Laxton"—that is, to residents only. Again, the ritual ends with refreshments at that aviary of activity, the Dovecote Inn.

Why this system of agriculture survived at Laxton is uncertain. That it will continue to survive is more certain, for the Minister of Agriculture is now lord of the manor.

A minister of castles might have saved the castle. Nottinghamshire castles are in general disappointing, for most have only the green mound remaining. Although this is true of the Laxton castle, it is nevertheless perhaps the best surviving example in the county of the motte-and-bailey type of Norman castle. A motte is the steep mound which forms the main feature of eleventh- and twelfth-century castles, and a bailey is the open space or court of a fortified castle. The mount of Laxton castle, with a circumference of 816 feet and a slope of 71 feet, was surrounded by an inner bailey of nearly eight acres. A short grassy walk from opposite the church leads to the remains of the ground plan.

Only the imagination can conjure up the splendid castle built soon after the Norman Conquest by the de Caux family, with an all-around view including Lincoln Cathedral some twenty-four miles away. Any disappointment that is felt may be tempered by two bonuses. First, the castle mound offers a close-up view of the fields. Second, it offers a distant view of the village and the dominating church.

The large, thirteenth-century Church of St. Michael went through a

Gargoyles on Church of St. Michael

period of neglect and abuse in the eighteenth century when it was actually strewn with rubbish. Then those well-meaning Victorians "restored" it. The early English tower was dismantled together with the last bay of the nave. A new tower was erected and the nave shortened by one bay, thereby destroying the proportions of the building. Nevertheless, it has features of great architectural beauty and age such as the magnificent nave clerestory,

73

the tall and slender circular piers of the nave arcade, a fourteenth-century font, and the north aisle screen of 1532. Among the gargoyles to be found outside are grotesque animals, a cross-legged satyr, and a crouching man.

Inside are tombs of the Everingham and Lexington families, lords of Laxton from the thirteenth to fifteenth centuries. Of particular interest is an attractive monument of Sir Adam de Everingham of 1335 and an oak effigy of his second wife, the only surviving wooden medieval effigy in the county.

Even more interesting (at least to Americans) is a permanent exhibition in the south aisle by local school children depicting village history. In a case containing an assortment of models, pictures, and memorabilia, is a notice attached to the Declaration of Independence announcing that Laxton is also called Lexington. "The Lexington in America Massachusetts," it continues, "is called after this Laxton."

Evidence that Lexington, in Massachusetts, was named for Laxton is mainly circumstantial. Originally known as "Cambridge Farms," the New England town was incorporated under the new name of Lexington in 1713. Since most of the towns in Massachusetts were named by the early settlers for the towns in England from which they emigrated, it is reasonable to suppose that this practice applied to Lexington as well.

It is extremely likely that settlers came from Laxton or the area. The nearby village of Scrooby is known, when it is remembered at all, for its Anglo-American ties. Postmaster William Brewster, born in 1566 in Scrooby, was a leader of the Separatist congregation which met at his home. Members of the group came from the surrounding cluster of villages and included the famous diarist, William Bradford. This spirited band of Separatists, forced to flee to Holland, later became the group of Pilgrim Fathers who sailed to the New World in 1620. Naturally, they continued to feel the old world ties strongly.

Some historians claim that the newly-incorporated Massachusetts town was named for Lord Lexington. But since the title emanated from the manor of Lexington (Laxton), it is clear that the name of the town in New England derives one way or another from the small town in Old England.

Some cynics say that the English save everything and discard nothing. They've even preserved an ancient system of farming which managed to survive through centuries of vast social and economic changes. Well, the American Lexington has preserved in its name the reminder of the remainder of an ancient past, a tribute to a living museum. To complete the circle begun by those earlier Pilgrims, how appropriate it would be for modern pilgrims to see the source and perhaps cap the visit with a stop at the Dovecote Inn. A refreshing anachronism in modern times is Saxon Laxton.

74

Leominster

Once upon a time, hurricanes did happen in Herefordshire—at least in the sense of stormy history. Located as it is in the Welsh Borderland, in a defensive position near the confluence of the Rivers Lugg and Arrow, Leominster found itself in the center of many upheavals.

Under the rule of the Saxon King Offa, a huge earthwork known as Offa's Dyke was built in 782 as a frontier line designed to give a measure of security to Leominster people who were in constant danger of raids from Wales. Part of Offa's Dyke can still be seen at Lyonshall, about ten miles west of Leominster.

The ninth century marks the beginning of severe struggles with the Danes; their armies ravaged the country, sometimes as a joint venture with the Welsh. It is believed that a Benedictine nunnery at Leominster was destroyed by the Danes in 980.

After the Norman Conquest of 1066, many castles were built on the borders of Wales, and a period of relative peace ensued during William's reign. But with the death of William the Conqueror, the Welsh resumed their incursions into England.

In one of the worst pillaging raids on Leominster, in 1207, the town was severely plundered and burned and nearly totally destroyed. To fight off invasions from Wales, castles were continuously being built, particularly through the twelfth and thirteenth centuries.

The Priory Church dates from the eleventh century and still stands as a link to the early history of Leominster. The first religious establishment was founded in 660 with Ealfred, a Northumbrian missionary as the first abbot. According to legend, the hungry Ealfred was eating bread when an equally hungry lion approached. Ealfred offered bread to the ferocious animal whose meek acceptance was taken as a certain sign that Ealfred would succeed in his work among the pagans. According to some, the legend of the lion is preserved in the name of the town, "Leonis Monasterium." More likely is the theory that Leominster referred to the "church of the nuns" or that "Leofminstre," as it appears in Domesday Book, is a contraction of Leofric's Minster; Leofric, Earl of the Mercians and husband of Lady Godiva, had endowed a nunnery here, which replaced the earlier one destroyed by the Danes. Little is known of his nunnery, which was disbanded in 1046.

The Priory was given in 1123 to the Benedictine monks of the Abbey of Reading. So Leominster was a daughter house of Reading Abbey and subject to it. Prosperous years followed, and the church was rebuilt and extended in the thirteenth and fourteenth centuries. The town prospered too with the making of quality woolen cloth. The famous fine wool was called "Lemster Ore." Poets have praised it, and the seventeenth-century poet Michael Drayton, who went so far as to compare it with the mythical Golden Fleece, wrote:

Where lives the man so dull on Britain's furthest shore
To whom did never sound the name of Lemster Ore,
That with the silkworm's thread for smallness doth compare.

Herrick wrote of a "bank of moss more soft than the finest Lemster Ore."

Alas, the Priory was destroyed with the Dissolution of 1539. The whole eastern end of the priory, including the central tower, was demolished. But the naves survived to be used as the parish church.

Seen today, the Priory Church of St. Peter and Paul, with its three naves, has just a portion of its former beauty. The Norman north nave has huge pillars, sixteen feet in circumference, and a thirteenth-century wall painting of the wheel of life. The central nave, built as a parish church in 1239, has a marvellous Perpendicular west window of a later date. The south aisle was added in the early fourteenth century.

Leominster remained a flourishing wool town until the Industrial Revolution, when the wool industry moved to the north.

Today, the principal industry of the area is agriculture, and Hereford cattle are exported all over the world from Leominster. Now, it is a quiet little market town with a population just over seven thousand, friendly and filled with plenty of picturesque old houses. Indeed, a profusion of timber-framed buildings make Leominster a wonderfully rich black-and-white town.

Draper's Lane, too narrow for cars, is an almost unspoiled pedestrian street which opens into Corn Square with a varied blending of architectural styles. The Friday Market fills the space in the square, and a walk leading past Lloyds Bank goes to the Grange, a beautiful green with the town's ancient earthworks running along the edge. At the east end is Grange Court, now used for municipal offices.

The Grange Court is a main architectural highlight of the town. Designed in 1633 by John Abel, the King's Carpenter, the lower level of this distinctive structure was originally the market for butter and eggs. But the open space between Ionic columns has been filled in, and above it rests the half-timbered upper floor. Because Grange Court was deemed a traffic hindrance, it was dismantled in the nineteenth century and re-erected in its present position.

76

Grange Court

Numerous other buildings of unusual interest exist. Forbury Chapel, built on the priory grounds in 1282, has a unique hammerbeam roof and a somewhat incongruous current use as an auction hall.

The Chequers Inn of 1600, the White Lion Inn of the early sixteenth century, the sixteenth-century Townsend House, the fourteenth-century Grafton House, and numerous Georgian houses are also distinctive. In addition, the Leominster Museum offers a variety of items of local interest.

Two nearby National Trust houses are open to the public. Eye Manor, erected in 1680 by a Barbados slave trader, is notable for its fine plaster ceilings, secret passage, and lovely gardens. The late eighteenth-century Berrington Hall has extensive grounds laid out by Capability Brown.

Five miles northwest of Leominster is Croft Castle, a Welsh border castle mentioned in Domesday Book; it is a reminder that this was once a land of turbulence in a time when many castles were built along the border for protection against raids.

If anyone emigrated from the finally peaceful and lovely land of Leominster to settle and name that other Leominster in America, the facts cannot be definitively traced. Nevertheless, there is more than a tacit relationship between the only two Leominsters known. An oil painting in the church suggestive of the surrounding countryside and entitled "Apple Blossoms" was a gift from Leominster, Massachusetts, in June 1976 in "the Bicentennial Year of the U.S.A. and the Thirteenth Centenary of the Diocese of Hereford."

Friendly Lemster (as the locals still pronounce it) is set in a beautiful valley among hopfields and apple orchards and lands in which plum-red Hereford cattle graze. Old timbered houses, market towns, and black-and-white villages add to the feeling of beauty and peace of the county. Indeed, hurricanes and harrowing history hardly ever happen.

Lincoln

The Cathedral of Lincoln dominates the city and the surrounding countryside. Situated high on a hill, the honey-colored stone cathedral is a spectacular sight from far or near. "A poem in architecture," it has been called. And Ruskin says that it is the best piece of architecture in the British Isles. The facade is richly decorated with a sculptured frieze over three elaborate Norman arches. A central tower of 271 feet is surpassed in height in England by the spires of Salisbury and Norwich. But in sheer beauty, many would agree, the cathedral is surpassed by none.

A previous cathedral, begun just half a dozen years after the Norman Conquest, was destroyed first by a fire of 1141 and then by an earthquake of 1185. In 1192, Bishop Hugh began work on the present and impressive three-towered cathedral, work which continued after his death in 1200 until its completion in about the year 1235. But his death brought about a further and major renovation. The Angel Choir at the east end was built between 1260 and 1280, replacing the apse end of the previous design, in order to accommodate crowds of pilgrims who came to visit the tomb of the canonized Bishop, St. Hugh. Dubbed the Angel Choir because of the number of carved angelic figures, it made a suitable setting for the Saint's shrine. Thirty figures of angels in spandrels of the arches perform a variety of activities. Here, one reads a scroll, there one holds up sun and moon in his hands; many play instruments.

There too, in the choir, on one of the corbels, sits the famous Lincoln Imp. Cross-legged, wide-mouthed, elfin-eared, a reminder of the less angelic aspect of life, he is a major attraction. In any case, with the magnificent Angel Choir, the cathedral was complete and completely magnificent.

Lincoln Imp

Lincoln Cathedral

Edward I and his Queen attended the dedication ceremony in 1280. Queen Eleanor died just a few years later, at Harby, ten miles from Lincoln, and her monument is in the Angel Choir. Lincoln had the first of a series of twelve memorial crosses erected by a heartbroken Edward I to mark each resting place on the journey from Harby Church to Westminister, where she was finally buried. Here too, in the Angel Choir, is the interesting tomb of Robert Fleming, founder of Lincoln College, Oxford. Underneath his effigy on the upper tier is a skeleton reproduction, a reminder of the ephemeral nature of life.

In the spacious interior, the nave is highlighted by dark Purbeck marble columns and by a twelfth-century font of black Tournai marble, embellished with figures of grotesque animals. The transept has stained-glass windows of the thirteenth and fourteenth centuries at either end. A kaleidoscope of colors in the round window at the southern end is called the Bishop's Eye. An attractive medallion window known as the Dean's Eye is in the other end of the transept.

The Cathedral Treasury contains one of the four original surviving copies of the Magna Carta. A thirteenth-century cloister on the north side leads to the library designed by Sir Christopher Wren and to the polygonal Chapter House, a graceful, thirteenth-century building with flying buttresses and single central pillar. Nearby, in the *yard* (a Saxon name for the precinct of a cathedral), is a statue of Alfred, Lord Tennyson, who was born in 1809 at nearby Somersby.

The Seamen's Chapel of Lincoln Cathedral has modern stained-glass windows which commemorate Lincolnshire people who influenced the history of America. Specific reference is made to "Captain John Smith, founder of the Colony of Virginia and prime mover of the establishment of New England." Many of the Pilgrim Fathers who sailed in 1620 came from Lincolnshire villages, particularly around Gainsborough. In 1754, when Lincoln, Massachusetts, became a town, it was given its name at the persuasion of the Honorable Chambers Russell, whose ancestors came from Lincolnshire.

Also on the hilltop, with its east gate facing the cathedral, is the Lincoln Castle. William the Conqueror ordered its erection in 1068. The Normans understood the strategic advantage of this site overlooking town activities and the River Witham, for they razed 166 houses in a kind of modern urbanization program to make room for the castle. The Observatory Tower, with an excellent view of the area from its top, was erected on a forty-foot high mound. The Lucy Tower was built on a second mound. A special attraction is the lovely oriel window in the Castle Gateway, removed from John of Gaunt's Palace for safety when that house was dismantled.

The view from the tower confirms that not only the Normans but all of the previous inhabitants of this hilltop site knew what they were doing when they chose the crest of this hill for settlement. Men have been living on the hill that is now Lincoln for some three thousand years. It had been settled in prehistoric times. Iron Age potsherds have been found as well as pre-Roman relics.

First called Caer-Lindcoit by Britons and then Linn-dun by the Celts, it was Latinized by the Romans to Lindum, which, like London, meant "the

Oriel Window in Castle Gateway

hill fort by the pool". Apparently, the part of the city below the hill was a stagnant pool or mere. The British root "lindos" meaning "marsh" persisted through the evolution of the name.

The Celtic settlement was replaced by the Romans and well settled by the Roman legionary fortress of Lindum by around 47 A.D. It was chosen as the site of a legionary fortress perhaps because of its accessibility to the sea and the narrowing of the River Witham and the need to watch over the marshes for the possibility of attackers from the north. By the end of the first century, it was made a *colonia* for the use of retired veterans of the legions and called Lindus Colonia. A carefully laid-out plan reveals the sewage system, aqueduct, buildings, streets, and colonnades of the very important walled

82

Newport Arch

town. Fragments of the walls remain. The Newport Arch, the north gate of Lindus Colonia, is unique in Britain. Traffic leaving the city via the main road to the north still goes through this Roman gateway.

Medieval Lincoln was equally important. It was appointed by the king as a Staple Town, a place for the public sale of wool. Here, merchants had to buy and sell. Wool shipped out of Lincolnshire had to pass through Lincoln, making the town wealthy.

That wealth is still in evidence in the twelfth-century town houses which still exist on a very steep hill named Steep Hill. It is an exciting street which leads from the town below to the cathedral and castle above.

The Jew's House is a stone building of the late twelfth century with rooms on the upper floor. It is located next door to the Jew's Court, also of this period, believed to have been the Jewish Synagogue and now a regional craft center. Further up the hill, Aaron's House is said to be one of the oldest inhabited dwellings in the land. This fine example of early domestic architecture belonged to an extremely wealthy figure. So great were his financial transactions, that when Aaron died in 1186, the king (who could always seize property of the Jews) had to expand the Exchequer to collect his debts. Belaset de Wallingford, a Jewess who later lived here, was hanged in 1290 for debasing coin. That was the year when Jews were expelled from England.

In the reign of Henry II, Jews had enjoyed a position of wealth and fame in Lincoln, but the Little St. Hugh episode which occurred in 1255 changed all of that. When the boy's dead body was discovered in a well, the Jews of Lincoln were blamed for his ritual murder. They were persecuted and many were executed. The boy was canonized and immortalized in legend. The story is recalled by Chaucer in "The Prioress's Tale." The shrine of Little St. Hugh in the south aisle of the cathedral is now accompanied with a disclaimer and apology for a totally discredited and shameful bit of Lincoln's past. It reads:

> Trumped up stories of 'Ritual Murders' of Christian boys by Jewish communities were common throughout Europe during the Middle Ages and even much later. These fictions cost many innocent Jews their lives.
> Lincoln had its own legend, and the alleged victim was buried in the Cathedral . . .
> Such stories do not redound to the credit of Christiandom, and so we pray:
> > Remember not Lord our offenses, nor the offenses
> > of our forefathers.

By the end of the fourteenth century, Lincoln was in decay. The wool trade was transferred thirty miles away to Boston, which had the advantage of direct access to the open sea. The wool rush was over, and the bustling, brilliant city of Lincoln became a dreary, dull town. Its history was marked by a series of recessions and disasters. Plague in the late sixteenth and early seventeenth centuries diminished the population. Devastation occurred in the Civil War. In 1724, Defoe described Lincoln as "dead, decayed and dirty."

But in the nineteenth century, new industry, a productive countryside, and the coming of the railways brought about an enormous expansion.

Lincoln today has its share of factories, chimneys, smoke, traffic, and rows of dull dwellings—the accoutrements of industrial society. But it contains also remnants of the past of endless variety and unceasing interest.

84

The Stonebow is a sixteenth-century gateway with the Guildhall situated above. High Bridge on the High Street, a medieval bridge lined with shops, has steps leading down to "Glory Hole" where original Norman stonework of the bridge can be seen.

The Norman church of St. Peter's at Gowts is further down the High Street, close to the Gowts (the Saxon word for channels or water-courses, as in *gut*). Another parish church with a Saxo-Norman tower, St. Mary-le-Wigford, has this amusing epitaph in the churchyard:

> Here lies, believe it if you can,
> Who though an attorney was an honest man

Stow, nine miles northwest, has a remarkable Saxon and Norman church which dates to the eleventh century. Further afield, twenty miles northwest, is Gainsborough, the St. Ogg's of George Eliot's *Mill on the Floss*.

Even when the visitor to Lincoln has started his tour, logically enough, with the cathedral, what better place to end than with the cathedral? For, like flickering fireplace flames, it fascinates with a warmth of ever-changing colors which vary with the changing time of day and with the seasons. Seen in brilliant morning sunshine, its honey-colored stone takes on a color that contrasts with the orange tints given by evening rays. On a gray day, it is different yet. Tones are altered and enhanced by the way the light is caught, and the viewer is caught and magnetized in turn. At night, floodlights illuminate the cathedral and give it still another character.

The City of Lincoln, like its cathedral, offers an endless array of sights. It is easy to despair of mastering all of the history and beauty of Lincoln; but that kind of despair can only be a source of joy.

Maldon

The road from London imparts a feeling of open space as it wends its way eastwards through the Essex countryside. The attractive agricultural landscape is occasionally broken by charming villages or country pubs, and an occasional farm house will announce the sale of free-range eggs or King Edward potatoes. Then, nine miles past Chelmsford, after a total distance of some forty miles—Maldon.

Maldon has evolved from a Saxon past—both the town and the name. It was Maeldune, the hill with a cross. Located in a picturesque part of Essex (a name derived from the East Saxons), the site was selected for its defensive position on a steep hill, above the broad estuary, at the mouth of the Blackwater.

Saxons and Danes vied for possession of the area. Edward the Elder successfully defended it against the Danes, defeating them in 920. But in the summer of 991, the Saxons were decisively defeated in the epic Battle of Maldon. The events were chronicled and immortalized in the contemporary Anglo-Saxon poem, "The Song of the Battle of Maldon," apparently written by a Saxon survivor. The Saxon leader Brythnoth was slain, and the Danes occupied the territory. Thus the Saxon journalist sang of the death of Brythnoth:

> . . . the grey-haired leader bade
> His men keep heart and onward press, good comrades undismayed.
> No longer could he stand upright, his eyes to heaven he bent.

Buildings of the Saxon period have survived in this area. One of the oldest churches in England still stands beside the sea where it was built in the seventh century. The chapel, fourteen miles east of Maldon in Bradwell-on-Sea, was built in 653 by St. Cedd, Bishop of the East Saxons. Actually, Bradwell has a curious mixture of old and new. The chapel stands by the remnants of a two-thousand year old Roman fort and a twentieth-century nuclear power station.

In the town itself, in Spital Road, is the ruin of St. Giles Leper Hospital, probably founded by Henry II in the twelfth century. In 1481 it was turned over to Beeleigh Abbey, about one mile from the town centre. The Abbey was founded in 1180 and largely destroyed at the Dissolution; the Chapter House is a remaining fragment that survives as an extremely attractive private house.

In the town center, near the top of the hill, is the Moot Hall, a pleasing brick structure with overhanging clock built in 1440 by Sir Robert D'Arcy.

Moot Hall

The Borough Council still meets here. A staircase leads from the Council Chamber to the roof, where there is a fine view of the Blackwater flowing and winding its way out to sea. Georgian buildings on High Street and Market Hill serve as reminders of thriving port days.

St. Mary's is a further reminder of former wealthy maritime trade. Located downhill by the waterside, near the Hythe (Saxon for wharf or landing place), it was built on a Saxon foundation and rebuilt around 1130. The Norman structure remains the basis of the present church. The lantern tower, with beacon to guide mariners, was rebuilt in 1636 and again in 1740.

Two ancient church towers dominate the Maldon skyline today—St. Peter's and All Saints'.

The fifteenth-century tower of St. Peter's still stands—just the tower. The church itself fell in 1665. The Plume library was erected up against the tower by Thomas Plume who also left his valuable collection of mainly theological and scientific books when he died in 1704. Among the five hundred volumes he donated are Dr. William Harvey's *Circulatione Sanguinis* of 1649 and a first edition of Milton's *Paradise Lost*.

All Saints' Church is nearby on the High Street. The Vicarage behind it is a charming fifteenth-century timber-framed house with ancient doorways and medieval paintings. But the oldest part of the church itself is its remarkable thirteenth-century west tower, with a triangular design that is the only one of its kind in England. Modern statues, in niches on the buttresses between the windows, are of such notables as St. Cedd (Bishop of the East Saxons), Brythnoth (slain Saxon hero of the famous battle), Sir Robert D'Arcy (whose fifteenth-century tower is now the Moot Hall), and Dr. Robert Plume (Archdeacon of Rochester and native of Maldon, who built the library which bears his name).

Inside, are monuments of people who could have made the Guinness Book of Records. Edward Bright weighed over six hundred pounds when he died in 1750. Billed as the "biggest man in England," special apparatus had to be fixed in the church to hold his coffin. A 1602 monument shows Thomas Crammock, a local tradesman, with his two wives and twenty-two children. Having eloped with his second wife, the couple escaped her father's hot pursuit by swimming their horses across the river to be married here in All Saints'.

But the feature for Americans is the Washington window, a gift given in 1928 by the citizens of Malden, Massachusetts, to the memory of Lawrence Washington, the great, great grandfather of George. Stained-glass scenes, glowing in color, include the landing of Columbus in America, the landing of the Pilgrim Fathers, and George Washington taking the oath of office as first President of the United States. This last English ancestor of George Washington, Rector of nearby Purleigh, lies buried in the churchyard.

Malden, Massachusetts, was settled in 1640 by Samuel Wayte and Joseph Hills and other emigrants from Maldon, Essex. They petitioned to have their spot in the wilderness, previously known as Charlestown, incorporated under the name of the place they left in England. In 1649, it became the Town of Maulden, located also in Essex, and went through several changes in spelling and growth to become a city in 1882.

Unlike the American Malden, the English Maldon has developed slowly.

The hill with a cross in Saxon times is now a crossroads of main highways. It is still a market town. It is still a trading and fishing port, and fishing boats still gather in Hythe Quay. It is still possible to have a pint of ale, or whatever, in the fourteenth-century Blue Boar, one of East Anglia's oldest inns. Built on a steep hill, the town continues to be perhaps the most picturesque and unspoiled in Essex.

Needham Market

The name of a town can be said to be an early written record of the place itself and a source of information. The Saxons gave the name of "Needham" to a home in need—that is, to a place of refuge. Seen today, it is a place in need of refurbishing. It is a scraggly town which straddles the main highway from Stowmarket to Ipswich. And if it once held an important market, there are no vestiges in the uninspired shops on the main street.

"Needham is but a poor Town," wrote the Reverend Thomas Cox in the 1720's in his revision of Camden's *Magna Britannia*. And Thomas Fuller said in 1662; "They are said to be in the Highway to Needham who haste to poverty." But when wool-combing was the staple industry, this little Suffolk town was well off, and the church is evidence of that.

Set alongside the main street, parallel with the road, the fifteenth-century Church of St. John the Baptist is made of flint and stone, the usual East Anglia materials. Its exterior is disappointing. But its interior is distinguished by a grand hammerbeam roof, generally accepted as one of the best in England.

Timber brackets, or hammerbeams, projecting out at right angles carry the arched braces which support the heavy weight of the roof. The need for a horizontal beam is thus eliminated, and a spectacular architectural effect is achieved. Here, the arched braces are concealed by a carved wood covering with angels, and angels also embellish the hammerbeam ends.

Called "the culminating achievement of the medieval carpenter" by Cautley in his *Suffolk Churches*, the remarkable roof is worth studying to figure out how it stays up, for it gives the final impression of a whole building suspended.

Needham Market has been loved by many for more than its church. Thomas James, born in Boston in Lincolnshire, was ejected from Needham in about 1661 under the Act of Uniformity, but apparently he and his family retained their fondness for Needham and its environs. His son Thomas, minister of Easthampton, Long Island, died in 1696, having stipulated that he be buried with his head pointing eastwards that he might face his people eternally.

Oxford

Oxford in Massachusetts has existed since 1683 when the settlement of Nipmuck was named for one of the greatest centers of learning in the world and the place where many Pilgrim Fathers had been educated. (This factor undoubtedly accounts for there being an Oxford also in Maine and in Connecticut.) But the new Oxford was largely settled by bands of French Huguenots seeking refuge from religious persecution. They gratefully retained the English name of their haven in the new world.

The first group of French settlers produced their own familiar names. A descendant of Pierre Beaudoin, James Bowdoin, became Governor of Massachusetts. Benjamin Faneuil was an ancestor of Peter Faneuil, that benefactor of Boston remembered by Faneuil Hall. Descendants of André Sigournais, the Sigourneys, are known in Boston and New England. The town is famous too as the home of Clara Barton, organizer of the American Red Cross. It is an interesting sidelight that the name of the neighboring town of New Roxbury was changed to Woodstock to parallel English geography which has the town of Woodstock as a neighbor to Oxford.

There, with the names, similarity ends. The city of Oxanforda dates to the eighth century with the founding of St. Frideswide's Nunnery. There is disagreement as to the origins of Oxford University, but a university was well established by the start of the thirteenth century and among the most important of the universities of Europe. Oxford is now a factory city with sprawling suburbs. But the heart of the city contains the colleges in an area of enormous interest and beauty.

A visit to it can probably only be superficial at best. Within a square mile area are listed 635 buildings of historical or architectural merit. In any case, highlights and pleasures of Oxford can be best derived by the simple means of looking—walking and looking. Unlike Cambridge with its open stretches of greenery and exposed buildings, in Oxford one has to go through gates and get behind walls to experience the scenes that emanate from a university so ancient that its founding date is unknown. Perhaps the sight that a see-er should encounter first is Radcliffe Square.

Radcliffe Square presents a scene of utter charm and harmony. The spire of St. Mary's can be seen from the center of the square, and visitors are permitted to climb the tower for the best view of Oxford. The Square is surrounded by the dull yellow buildings of Brasenose and Exeter on one side and by Hertford and All Souls on the other. The tall towers of All Souls add to the Oxford skyline. Dominating the picturesque scene is the dome of the

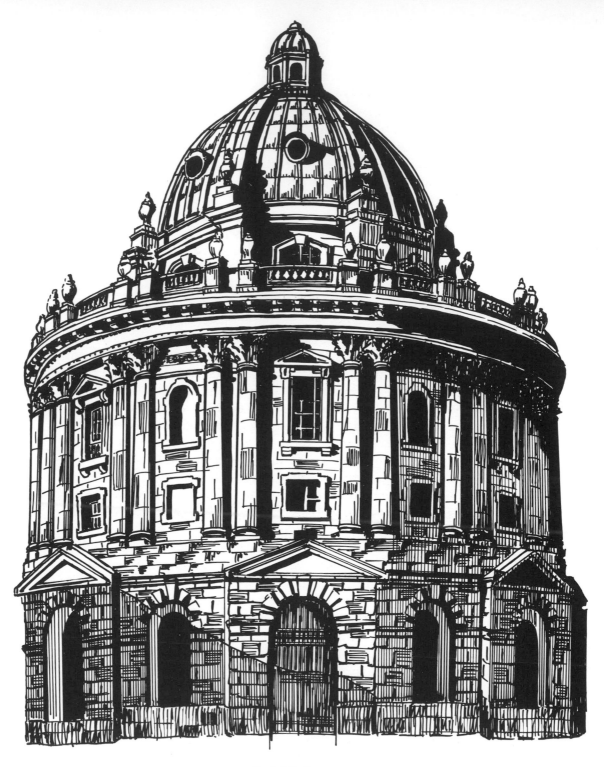

Radcliffe Camera

Radcliffe Camera. The Camera is a part of one of the world's largest libraries, the Bodleian, which completes another side of the square. It is affectionately known as "the Bodley" by undergraduates who can be seen scurrying in and out of the library buildings, no books under their arms, for the Bodley is not a circulating library. A visitor should find it easy to mingle and scurry too and become part of one of the most satisfying scenes in perhaps all of England.

In the Bodleian, visitors may view an engaging exhibition on the ground level which includes such literary finds as letters written by Virginia Woolf, George Bernard Shaw, John Masefield, Florence Nightingale; original manuscripts such as Kenneth Graham's *The Wind in the Willows;* Shakespeare's First Folio of 1623; memorabilia such as Shelley's guitar; and a variety of beautifully illuminated manuscripts. Upstairs near the Arts End is the most ancient part, the restored fifteenth-century Duke Humphrey's Library. The book shelves jut out into the room and form alcoves in which are the readers' desks; this arrangement was designed to take maximum advantage of natural lighting. Stained-glass windows and hushed whispers of attendants enhance the air of solemnity that pervades.

Nearby, at the end of Broad Street, is Sir Christopher Wren's Sheldonian Theatre, used for degree-giving ceremonies and other academic functions. There is a fine view from its cupola of the spires of Oxford and the streets below. The viewer can well appreciate that Oxford, subtitled a City of Spires, could accurately be retitled, a City of Aspiring Students.

Across the Broad is Blackwell's, the large book shop in Oxford which caters to students. It is proud of its tradition which permits the prospective buyer to browse unmolested. Its staff is eager to help, but only when requested to do so. Some fast readers have never had to buy any books! It's worth rambling through this enormous shop with its attractive displays even if it is not possible to leave without having succumbed to a purchase or two.

Next door to Blackwell's is Trinity College, notable for its fine baroque chapel, a quadrangle which was designed by Wren, and a magnificent garden, perennially viewed by the bust of a famous alumnus, Cardinal Newman.

Each of the thirty-eight colleges that comprise Oxford University has its own living quarters, chapel, dining hall, and library. While the basic features are similar, each takes on its own unique character. For example, University College, having existed since 1249, claims to be the oldest. Merton claims to have the oldest library. Trinity, to have the finest gardens. St. John's may have the largest lawn in Oxford, and Magdalen may be the most beautiful. But there is a basic plan, common to all.

Tom Tower, Christ Church College

The visitor enters each enclosed college through a gate at which is situated the porter's lodge. Beyond the lodge is a quadrangle, around which are the living quarters of the undergraduates, as students in Oxford are called. Larger colleges have additional quadrangles, and staircases lead to the actual living quarters. Generally, the undergraduate is given a two-room suite consisting of a bedroom and a sitting room or study. To make the environment even more conducive to productive study, he is also given a scout, as servants are known in Oxford. Visitors are welcome during the hours which are usually posted on a notice board at the porter's lodge. Beyond the gate are possibilities for delightful discoveries of all kinds. But diversions, too, are so easy to come by in Oxford.

94

The White Horse, a friendly pub situated on the Broad Street adjacent to Trinity, serves a variety of foods in addition to the usual thirst quenchers. If pubs are one's cup of ale, a favorite is located a bit further down the Broad off Holywell on Bath Place. In this very narrow lane is the Turf. Or, there is the Bear or Blue Boar.

Away from the college area, the Perch and the Trout, both on the Thames, are definitely worthwhile. The Perch, in Binsey, offers drinks and buffet and repose in a charming interior of old fireplaces and uneven floors. The Trout is a delightful country inn in Wolvercote, overlooking a small rushing waterfall and a peacock garden. A long, pleasant stroll or bicycle ride on a towpath along the Thames leads to both places.

With so much to do and see in Oxford, the task of selecting seems hopeless. However, here is one walking tour designed to convey at least the idea of the numerous wonders of this endlessly fascinating city.

After a morning's exercise in the library area, walk on New College Lane. You pass under a replica of the Venetian Bridge of Sighs which joins two buildings of Hertford. The Hertford College Bridge is a joyfully imaginative structure, an artistic triumph rather than a merely practical passage for two buildings of Hertford.

Continuing on New College Lane, you may want to enter the gate of New College, inappropriately named, for it is one of the oldest colleges. In one corner of the front quadrangle, with its circular area of grass, a staircase leads to the dining hall. The chapel, reached from another corner of the quadrangle, is memorable for its impressive seven-foot statue of Lazarus by Jacob Epstein, its stained-glass windows designed by Sir Joshua Reynolds, an El Greco painting of St. James, important brasses, and many relics and treasures including a magnificently-wrought Founder's Crozier. Near the chapel entrance, a passageway leads to the cloisters. In the solitude of this lovely, reposeful setting, it is easy to lose even the memory of the well-trafficked, bustling High Street.

Beyond the front quadrangle, an archway leads to an open quadrangle facing a garden bounded by the original old city wall. The wall still retains its arrow slits and steps leading to a wide top, designed originally for walking or marching on. But now weeds and wild flowers sprout from crevices.

But you return to the winding lane which leads on to High Street. While on the High Street, you ought to visit the thirteenth-century University College for one of the sights which will qualify you, if not to receive an Oxford degree, at least to leave the ranks of mere tourism. Visitors to Oxford learn that Alice's Wonderland emanated from Christ Church where the Reverend Charles Lutwidge Dodgson, better known as Lewis Carroll, first told the now familiar story to Alice Liddell, the third daughter of the then Dean of Christ Church. Not everyone, however, knows about the Shelley Memorial in University College. Originally planned for the poet's tomb in Italy, the monument now stands in a dome-roofed structure. The ornate base is made up of a gryphon on either end and a sedentary central bronze figure, the Muse of Poetry, sadly supporting her head. The reason for her dejection is uncertain since she, at least, does not have to look at this work of art. A sign at her feet announces simply, "Shelley." Otherwise, it might be difficult to believe that the prone white marble figure on the slab supported by this base is indeed the poet. He lies stretched out naked, on his side, one leg bent under the extended leg, in simulation of the drowned body that was washed ashore. The family of the poet rejected this memorial monument and the College accepted it. University College expelled the poet so long ago and is perhaps trying to make amends now for having rejected the poet then.

But the mention of Alice in Wonderland could cause still another digression to another memorable Oxford scene, Christ Church with its round Tom Tower, which might be considered the trademark of Oxford just as Big Ben is for London. The bell, "Great Tom," rings one hundred and one times at five minutes past nine every evening to indicate the curfew. Why one hundred and one? To commemorate the original number of students at Christ Church. Why five minutes *after* the hour? Situated five minutes away from Greenwich mean time, this was the original and accurate way of computing time.

The Broad Walk alongside this College leads to Rose Lane, the Botanic Gardens, and the area of High Street, where Magdalen College (pronounced Maudlin) is situated. So impressive is the Gothic Magdalen Tower, that Wren based his design for St. Michael's in London on it. A circular foot path begins beyond the cloistered quadrangle and winds its way through woods and alongside a deer park, streams, and the Cherwell River.

Assuming you have resisted all other temptations such as intriguing book stores, antique shops, clothing shops, or other colleges, now comes your opportunity to go punting on the Cherwell, a branch of the Thames (or Isis as it is known locally). The man who rents the elongated crafts known as punts will give a quick course in how to stand up on one end like a Venetian gondolier and balance precariously while steering and pushing your way through the water. Fun and competition come from swans and from other punters who are also mastering the technique.

Should your plans to go punting be drowned out by traditional English

Magdalen Tower

weather, there are always things of interest to be viewed indoors. But if there were no other reason to visit Oxford, if Oxford were somehow divested of its colleges and its students, the Ashmolean Museum would be sufficient justification for the fifty-mile trip from London. This Museum houses a vast collection of antiquities, Eastern art, astrolabes, tapestries, and paintings by such noted artists as Guardi, Tiepolo, Tintoretto, Uccello, Constable, Van Dyke.

The casual visitor can hardly begin to uncover the inexhaustible wonders of Oxford. Add to the city the innumerable attractions of the surrounding countryside—the Norman Church in the suburb of Iffley, Blenheim Palace, the Cotswolds, Stratford—and you're here for a long stay. Indeed, you can spend centuries seeing it all—and loving it!

Plymouth

The Pirates may have come from Penzance, but the Pilgrims did *not* come from Plymouth. Plymouth was the last port of call for the Pilgrim separatists only because of some bad luck. Although the Mayflower passengers were mainly from East Anglia, they had been settled for the past twelve years in Leyden in Holland. Now, on their way to the New World, the accompanying ship, the Speedwell, needed repairs; in Plymouth it was found to be unseaworthy and eventually left behind. Passengers dropped out or regrouped, and the Mayflower sailed on September 6, 1620, with a party of 102 aboard. The momentous occasion is commemorated in England by a plaque on the Barbican and in America by the naming of their settlement after the English town which treated them so well.

Actually, there are some forty Plymouths in various parts of the world, a fact which suggests that Plymouth was used as a taking-off point for many expeditions. Its coastal situation in the southwestern corner of Devon where it guards the English Channel gives Plymouth a position of great strategic importance. It became a center for voyages of exploration and discovery and for naval maneuvers as its sea power developed through the centuries.

Nine hundred years ago it was a small village with the ancient name of Sudtone—South Town. The ancient harbor is still called Sutton Harbor. And the oldest part of the city is around Sutton Harbor in an area known as the Barbican, which recalls that a barbican or outer fortification of the castle of Plymouth once existed.

Plymouth's history is based on the tradition of seamanship and shipbuilding that developed. In Norman times the Domesday village began to prosper as a fishing and trading port. Edward I was among the first to recognize its potential as a naval base. It was he who assembled a fleet of 325 ships in 1287 for the Bordeaux wars against Phillip of France. By the fourteenth century the descriptive name of Plymouth came to be used generally for the town situated near the mouth of the River Plym. The place had grown from a hamlet to the fourth town in the kingdom.

Plymouth thrived and grew rich during the years of the Spanish threat. Several sixteenth-century merchants' houses remain to attest to that earlier wealth. And the old character with narrow, winding, cobbled streets remains as well. The oldest street in Plymouth is New Street; it was new when it was laid out in Elizabethan times. The so-called Elizabethan House in New Street has been restored and is open to visitors.

This was the age of merchant-adventurers, explorers and pirates, with

Plymouth Harbor

some Elizabethans being all at one time. The Hawkins family led in the competition among merchant seamen to secure the wealthy new trade for themselves. The notorious John Hawkins organized one of the first large-scale slave trades, selling African natives to the Spaniards in the West Indies. Drake joined the ventures of the Hawkins family, to which he was related, in privateering, ventures of plunder, and illicit trading—all aimed against the Spanish, and therefore quite acceptable.

Sir Francis Drake is probably Plymouth's most notable celebrity. As a result of his exploits, he returned to Plymouth laden with enough Spanish gold to ingratiate himself into royal circles. And in 1577, he undertook his famous three-year voyage around the world.

The Hoe

His memorial statue enhances the wide grassy expanse overlooking Plymouth Sound known as the Hoe—a "hill" or "height." From this plateau high above the Barbican he watched for the approach of the Spanish Armada in 1588, an invasion designed by King Phillip of Spain to remove Elizabeth from her throne and establish Spanish dominance of the New World—the greatest danger England ever had to face again until 1940. The Hoe has a fine sea view and a fine bowling green, and there Drake played perhaps the most famous game of bowls in history as he waited for arrival of the vast

100

Armada. When word came to him, Drake is supposed to have answered that there was "plenty of time to finish the game and beat the Spaniards after." There was and he did. The cool, if legendary, statement was not mere idle boast. Plymouth was Drake's home port, and he knew that the British fleet could not move out of the Plym estuary for some hours, until the tide had turned. He defeated the Armada and has been immortalized by a grateful England.

Plymouth stood against Charles I in the Civil War of the 1640's. When Charles II came to the throne he built, in 1666, the Citadel. This fortification was designed not to defend England against foreign enemies but to intimidate the inhabitants he so completely distrusted. The northern side of the fortress has an abundance of gun ports and a commanding position of the town itself.

The Citadel dominates all of Plymouth from its position on the eastern heights of Plymouth's great attraction, the Hoe. Nearby is the Marine Biological Association with laboratory and aquarium. Also on the lovely stretch of greenery, on the west, is a cliff with panoramic views. The Eddystone lighthouse, fifteen miles out to sea, is visible. But Smeaton's lighthouse, on the eastern end of the Hoe, is, visitable. Originally, Smeaton's lighthouse had stood lighting the Channel from 1759 to 1882. But because the sea had undermined the rock on which it was standing, it was dismantled and re-erected on the Hoe.

Plymouth, the largest city in the West Country and the home of the Royal Navy, was very severely bombed in World War II, and its center is almost entirely new. It has been rebuilt with wide, modern streets and shopping centers. Armada Way has such fine new buildings as the Civic Center and Guildhall. The medieval Church of St. Andrew underwent a remarkably beautiful job of restoration with stained-glass windows in the east end by John Piper and a memorial window in the west to Lord Astor; he and his American-born wife helped enormously in the rebuilding of Plymouth. But many authentic old bits of Plymouth remain. The fifteenth-century Prysten House behind the Church was probably the home of the monks of Plympton Priory before the Dissolution of the Monasteries, when they had control of the area. The Church of St. Budeaux on the outskirts of the city is the place where Sir Francis Drake married Mary Newman. There is the Citadel, of course. And the tiny streets around the harbor remain unchanged.

Plymouth has treated its visitors well. One notable arrival took place on October 2, 1501, when the fifteen-year old daughter of Ferdinand and Isabella, Katherine of Aragon, landed at Plymouth to be married to Prince Arthur. The town cheered her. She stayed for two weeks and never returned.

Indeed, the ill-fated princess might well have wished she had never seen England at all, for in November of 1501 she was married in London to Prince Arthur and widowed within five months. Her troubles began when she became the wife of his younger brother Henry VIII and the first of his six queens.

Pocahontas, the beautiful Indian girl who had saved the life of Captain John Smith, landed in Plymouth in June, 1616. She was about twenty when she and her husband, an English widower and tobacco planter, John Rolfe, came to Plymouth. She was lionized, taken up and entertained by fashionable social circles until, alas, the English climate undermined her health. She died of consumption in 1617.

In 1762, the painter Sir Joshua Reynolds, who came from Plymouth, hosted Dr. Johnson on a visit of Plymouth of several weeks. Dr. Johnson is reported to have gorged himself on tea and Devon cream and to have enjoyed the visit enormously. He too was highly honored by Plymouth society.

In 1772, James Cook departed from Plymouth on his circumnavigation of the world. And in recent times, in 1966, Sir Francis Chichester sailed from here on his single-handed journey around the world.

With all of these comings and goings, by sea and by land, Plymouth can be a good host. Thousands of visitors come every year from overseas. The Pilgrim Fathers were "kindly entertained and courteously used by divers friends there dwelling," says the bronze tablet on the Barbican. And Plymouth continues to extend kind entertainment and courtesy to modern-day pilgrims whether they arrive to play bowls on the Hoe or to pay homage to the past.

St. Albans

St. Albans in Vermont has as its namesake a city that is some two thousand years old. St. Albans in England is a thriving city about twenty miles north of London, known for its great cathedral, intriguing streets, old inns, markets, parks, and the remains of the Roman city of Verulamium

St. Albans derives its name from the first Christian martyr in Britain. Alban, a Roman soldier stationed in Verulamium, was converted from paganism by a fugitive Christian priest whom he sheltered and helped to escape. For his new faith, Alban was condemned to death in the year 209. A church was built on the site of his martyrdom, and the shrine still stands in what has evolved to become, in 1877, a cathedral.

One good way to get the sense of a place is by viewing it, whenever possible, from a high perspective. In St. Albans, the panorama can be viewed from the centrally-located Clock Tower. This striking edifice (which also strikes the hours) was originally built as a curfew tower between 1403 and 1412. It houses a still older bell, cast in 1335, which can be seen from the winding stone stairs which lead to the top. The top affords a view of historic Watling Street, built by the Romans as a main route to connect the bustling city of Verulamium to another important Roman city, Londinium. On the western edge of St. Albans, Verulamium Park contains the ruins of that first-century Roman town and comprises most of the area of the old Roman city. On market days, one may also witness the colorful scene beyond French Row, a charming street to the west of the tower, which imparts the feeling of a medieval town. Here were quartered the French soldiers of the Dauphin of France sent for by the barons to force King John to adhere to Magna Carta. Nearby Holywell Hill is lined with Georgian houses and named for the legendary Holly Well; the father of King Arthur used its waters to heal the wounds he incurred in battle with the Saxons. The Waxhouse Gate, directly across High Street from the tower, is a covered passageway leading to the Cathedral and Abbey Church. In this archway, candles were sold to pilgrims on their way to the shrine of the saint.

In the cathedral, the shrine is a remarkably skillful restoration of the original, which was smashed to pieces during the reign of Henry VIII, at the time of the Dissolution of the Monasteries. A nearby watching chamber guards the shrine. Only two such structures exist, the other being in Christ Church, Oxford.

The church itself has been restored, rebuilt, enlarged, and endlessly altered to result in the existing structure. The dates of origin are sobering.

The Clock Tower

The pillars in the south transept, Saxon in origin, were incorporated into the present church by the Normans. The impressive Norman tower, the transept, the choir, the bays of the north side of the nave were built between 1077 and 1088 from bricks taken from Verulamium down in the valley. Standing in the long nave, one can still get an impression of what the Norman nave must have looked like. Massive piers and rounded arches are the chief architectural features here. Colored murals and designs, dating from about 1215, were recently uncovered after centuries of hidden existence under whitewash.

Outside, the fourteenth-century Abbey Gatehouse is the work of Abbot

104

Ye Old Fighting Cocks Inn

Thomas de la Mare whose reign marks the high point of the monastery. The Gatehouse is the single surviving monastic building. The Abbot de la Mare used the Gatehouse as a prison, and subterranean dungeons have confined inmates from his time to the Napoleonic Wars and beyond. Today, its inmates are students of St. Albans School, one of the oldest public schools in the country.

On the way to Verulamium, in Abbey Mill Lane, is the charming "Ye Old Fighting Cocks Inn." Originally the fishing lodge of the monastery, it later became, as the name implies, a cock-fighting center. The Fighting Cocks claims to be one of the "oldest inhabited licensed houses in England." Founded in 795, it suggests a history as interesting as its octagonal shape and makes a perfect stop for repast before continuing on to Verulamium.

Verulamium Park contains the ruins which mark the grandeur that was Rome. Excavations have been going on for the past twenty-five years, and the initial view of remnants of the original city wall is indeed impressive. From the archeological remains and a little imagination, one can conjure up a picture of the ancient Roman city. It consisted of a forum, streets of houses and shops, two temples, two triumphal arches, and a theatre. The Roman Theatre, not an amphitheatre, was the largest in the country. It continues to be unique, for it is the only Roman theatre open to view in Britain.

A Hypocaust, in relatively good condition, is a tribute to Roman ingenuity in coping with a need which still plagues inhabitants of Britain—a central heating system to contend with English weather. The suite of heated or "hypocaust" rooms, used for bathing, constituted the wing of a private town house. The warming room of this suite features a large mosaic.

The Saxon St. Michael's Church is notable for its warmth of character and for its effigy of St. Albans' most illustrious resident, Francis Bacon. It stands on the site of the Roman Basilica where Alban received trial and sentence before being led to his execution. The nearby Museum, in the area where formerly stood shops and houses of the Roman forum, contains mosaics and various artifacts found in the area. A Dolphin mosaic and painted walls of one large town house are displayed.

Patterns emerge. The thriving and industrial St. Albans of today was also an active and industrial city then. Centuries earlier, it was a manufacturing center for pottery as evidenced by the archeological find of a pottery dump. One wonders whether Verulamium might have been the site of the first factory reject shop.

Verulamium Park, by the River Ver, provides long, interesting walks and a site for contemplation. With the passage of time, the population gradually resettled in the area of the shrine. As Verulamium declined, the town of St. Albans flourished and expanded to become a great city and not just the relic of a once-great city.

A final view of St. Albans from the valley below symbolizes this movement through the centuries. Look across the lake, formerly the monks' fishpond, at the upper portions of the cathedral. There is the imposing Norman tower, built of bricks which were once part of Verulamium.

And if imagination is allowed to run rampant, look across the ocean too, to the smaller, newer St. Albans which was inspired by this Hertfordshire city in Old England—to St. Albans, New England.

Sandwich

Once the most important port in England, Sandwich is now a small town in Kent on the River Stour some two miles inland from the sea.

The town was probably founded after the Romans departed from Britain in mid-fifth century. They left behind the nearby Richborough Castle, or Rutupiae as the Romans called it, the first Roman base in Britain after the invasion by Claudius in 43 A.D. The fortification is one of the most impressive Roman ruins in the country.

Deriving its name from the Saxon "Sand-wyk"—the village or settlement on the sand—Sandwich became a great port, one of the original Cinque Ports. Of the original five ports, Hastings is now a prosperous seaside resort. Dover has become, with the building of a great artificial harbor, one of the main ports on the English Channel. New Romney is a somewhat decayed but pretty inland village. Hythe is another holiday resort. Only Sandwich remains a lively little market town, an enchanting place in this southeastern corner of England, which still conveys a sense of its past.

The purpose of the Cinque Ports was to supply the King of England with ships and men for fighting his wars—a kind of navy. In return, the ports received certain privileges. In effect, they were little sovereign states with their own rights and courts and with freedom from taxation by the Crown.

The Cinque Ports confederation was formed for mutual support in the reign of Edward the Confessor (1042-1066). Rye and Winchelsea were designated "Ancient Towns" and added to the confederation to alleviate the strain of providing for the needs of the king. Towns which joined later were known as "Limbs." Sandwich was most important, and royalty frequently stayed here.

The wars with France kept Sandwich Haven (as the port was called) busy. Here ships gathered between 1203 and 1216 to try to recapture the lands lost to France by King John. The victorious Battle of Sandwich was fought in 1217 and is still remembered by the Hospital of St. Bartholomew, built to commemorate the victory. Another crucial conflict took place in 1293 when the Cinque Ports demolished the French fleet. The fifteenth century saw a reversal of fortune with several severe attacks by the French. In 1457, an expedition from Honfleur inflicted serious damage and resulted in the deaths of so many of its citizens including the Mayor, that the Mayor of Sandwich still wears a black gown as the official robe.

The supremely important Haven of Sandwich began to deteriorate by 1500 because of silting up of the mouth of the river. Indeed, nature was winning a war against all of the ports, and by the time Henry VIII came to the throne, the days of greatness of the Cinque Ports and their subsidiaries were over. Henry VIII, anxious about the plight of the port, visited Sandwich in 1532 and again in 1539. Elizabeth I visited in 1573 and was petitioned to improve the harbor. However, nothing could be done to save it. Silting was leading inexorably to the end of Sandwich as a port.

Eventually, in 1890, the land which covered the former flourishing port became one of the finest seaside golf courses anywhere. Today, only Dover is a functioning port, and it alone retains a link to former maritime glory.

A certain Cape Cod town retains a link to glorious, old Sandwich. In 1634, a shipload of 102 persons, including twenty-four adults and twenty-one children from Sandwich, embarked at the ancient port for the American plantations of New England. Five years later, the General Court in Boston allowed the original Indian name of the Cape Cod settlement to be replaced with the name of Sandwich.

Another linking is interesting, if irrelevant. A descendant of the first Earl of Sandwich, a compulsive gambler, took his meals in the form of some bit of food inserted between two slices of bread in order not to interrupt his game. Although he had no connection to the town, Sandwich was immortalized in a word now known throughout the world.

The ancient town has itself been given a kind of immortality. The whole of the old town within the original defenses has been designated a conservation area, thus ensuring that the exceptional number of valuable and attractive timbered buildings will be preserved. The old part is the same area as that within the medieval walls; and the population of five thousand is not significantly higher than it was in Elizabethan times.

Earth ramparts follow the line of the old wall which encircled the town and provide a pleasant tree-lined walk around much of the town. The maze of narrow streets and alleys within is filled with a jumble of old houses and cottages. The mixture of medieval, Tudor, and Georgian buildings have paneled walls, oak beams, or plaster-work ceilings. Many have cellars which once had the legitimate purpose of storing wine and then the illegitimate purpose of hiding smuggled goods.

In Strand Street are the best of the timbered houses. Near St. Mary's, behind a brick front, is the King's House where Henry VIII and Queen Elizabeth I lodged. The datestone of 1713 is deceptive, for the brickwork of that date conceals a timber-framed house of about 1400. The Pilgrims and the Weavers are other fine examples of fifteenth-century houses. The thirteenth-century Long House, fifty-two feet long, was once known as Herring House, for this was the place where herring dues were paid. At the

The Fisher Gate

end of Upper Strand Street is a splendid house named the Salutation, designed by Sir Edwin Lutyens in Wren style.

The riverside Strand Street leads to a bridge and ancient barbican before opening on to the quay. The Barbican Gate of 1539, with its twin turrets, collects tolls from traffic crossing the bridge over the River Stour. The Fisher Gate on the quay is even older—1384. Nearby, is the old Customs House, marred by an eighteenth-century brick facade covering the medieval timber-framed house.

In the heart of Sandwich, in the Market Square, is the Guildhall of 1579. An oak-paneled Court Room is on the ground floor. The Council Chamber above is hung with portraits of such notables as Edward Montagu, the first Earl of Sandwich; one of England's great naval heroes, he may have meant to compliment the town by adopting its name for his title. The Guildhall also maintains a small but rich collection of objects of local history including original charters and documents.

St. Peter's in the center of Sandwich near the Guildhall, is one of three surviving medieval churches. Its clock on the tower can be seen from almost every part of town. The curfew bell has rung from St. Peter's every evening at eight since the thirteenth century. But formerly it proclaimed the time for releasing hogs on to the streets to scavenge. Nowadays, although the job of refuse disposal is done by dustmen (when they're not on strike), the bell nevertheless continues to ring.

St. Mary's was left in derelict condition when it was damaged by an earthquake in 1578 and a collapsed tower in 1667. But it has recently been restored, and some Norman work remains in the west end.

St. Clement's is the parish church and the largest and most important of the three. Its pure Norman tower, massive and elaborately embellished with three rows of arcading, dates to 1100 and is perhaps the finest in England. Inside are richly carved choir stalls, a magnificent fifteenth-century font adorned with heraldic shields, and monuments of the prosperous members of the medieval community. In the chancel is an unusual feature—a medieval system of sound amplification consisting of holes in the stone below the choir stalls and a similar set of holes high up on the sanctuary walls.

Sandwich has no stupendous monuments. But the meanderer is easily rewarded at nearly every step. Quaint old houses are everywhere. In King Street, the Dutch House is an excellent example of houses built in the style of their homeland by Dutch refugees who fled from Spanish oppression to Sandwich in the 1560's, bringing their weaving skills with them and adding to the prosperity of the town.

110

Norman Tower of St. Clement's

A plaque on a small house in New Street marks the place where Thomas Paine lived in 1759. He is proudly remembered for the single year he spent in Sandwich before he left for America and published his revolutionary writings.

Outside the town wall just off the Dover Road is the medieval Hospital of St. Bartholomew, an ancient almshouse with a beautiful thirteeenth-century chapel, erected to commemorate the Battle of Sandwich fought in 1217 on

St. Bartholomew's Day, the 24th of August. The hospital founded in honor of the saint still functions as a charity for the needy. Tradition is strong. Each Saint's Day, the practice continues of distributing Bartlemas biscuits stamped with the hospital seal and founding year of 1190; in fact, food and lodging were provided here for pilgrims as far back as that original date.

Sandwich today ought to be slowly savored for the endless tidbits it offers—green walks along the ramparts, an ancient fresh water channel made in 1287 known as the Delf flowing under ancient houses, narrow and intriguing lanes . . . the story of some thirteen centuries. Countless bits unite to make a caviar Sandwich.

Happily, the edible pun can be carried to an extreme in England: Sandwich in Kent can be coupled with Brown Bread Street in Sussex, With Ham in Wiltshire, and Beer in Devon.

Springfield

The parish of Springfield, as seen today, gives the appearance of a tiny, attractive village or suburb of Chelmsford

Oliver Goldsmith is believed to have lived in Springfield for a time while he wrote his "Deserted Village." Although the grounds are thin that Springfield is the prototype for that poem, it can be viewed as the source of inspiration.

Church of All Saints

The heart of any English village is its church, and the Church of All Saints, largely Norman, has a delightful setting among tall trees beside a village green. Among the many items of interest inside the church are its unusual fourteenth-century window tracery, mid-thirteenth-century carved font, medieval stained glass, memorial brass of 1421 of a man in armor, a fifteenth-century chancel screen, and a Tudor funeral helm. Of particular

113

historical interest to Americans is an ancient tablet listing church wardens. Among the names inscribed is that of William Pynchon, a resident of Springfield who sailed with the Pilgrim Fathers.

One of the original incorporators of Massachusetts Bay, Pynchon led a group of emigrants from Roxbury in 1636 to the wilderness of the west on the banks of the Connecticut River. His settlement was the first in the western part of what was to become Massachusetts. Within a few years, the settlers secured official status as a town, and the name of Springfield replaced the original Indian name of Agawam to honor the English home of their founder.

Although Pynchon was successful as a trader, he ran into trouble with a book he wrote on his religious beliefs, "The Meritorious Price of Our Redemption." Printed in London, the book, which expressed views contrary to official dogma, was condemned and publicly burned in Boston. Thus, Pynchon may have been the first to be banned in Boston. Dishonored and removed from his position as judge at Springfield, he returned to England in 1652.

Despite his unhappy experience in the early history of the New World, William Pynchon's role in later history is vital, for he is remembered as the founder of the now great industrial city of Springfield in Massachusetts, a city which stands in complete contrast to the quiet, hardly noticeable parish of Springfield in Essex.

Sudbury

The old Saxon town of "Suthburgh," the fortified town in the south, has retained the essence of its ancient name and character. Sudbury is first mentioned in the Anglo-Saxon Chronicle of 797, although the date of the actual founding is not known. The town was surrounded by a moat which is marked in modern Sudbury by Friars Street, one of the attractive winding streets which leads out from the market square.

Sudbury has had a weekly market since Saxon days, as mentioned in the Domesday Book of 1086. The town is still vibrant with activity on Thursdays, when open stalls in the open space of Market Hill purvey a variety of produce and goods. Although Sudbury has a modern shopping precinct which attracts people from all around, it is Market Hill that is magnetic, particularly on market days.

In this focal point of Sudbury is a statue of the town's most illustrious citizen and one of England's greatest painters, Thomas Gainsborough. The house in Sepulchre Street in which he was born in 1727 still stands. It is open to the public as a museum, and the street is now called Gainsborough Street. Appropriately, it runs into Market Hill, where the bronze statue of the beloved painter, palette in hand, stands in front of the west door of St. Peter's Church and overlooks the bustling scene.

St. Peter's has become a redundant church. Built in the fifteenth century, it is being used for concerts and public functions. All around the open square are other noteworthy buildings. On the south side is the public library, formerly the Corn Exchange. To the north of the church is the grey brick Town Hall of 1828. An attractive Georgian house contains Lloyds Bank.

Interesting old buildings exist everywhere in Sudbury. The Chantry is a timbered and gabled house on Stour Street with a finely carved corner post. Next to it is Salter's Hall, the home of a fifteenth-century merchant and the most elaborate of the timbered houses surviving in Sudbury. Also of the fifteenth century is the old Moot Hall, with a pretty oriel window and overhanging story. A fifteenth-century gate is all that remains of the Dominican Priory built in 1272 and dismantled at the Dissolution of the Monasteries by Henry VIII. The Ship and Star is a four-hundred year old inn which may have been a pilgrim's guest house for the neighboring priory.

These ancient timbered houses and fine old churches are evidence of the wealthy wool trade which once characterized Sudbury. Keeping the past while adapting to the future, Sudbury still carries on an important weaving industry, especially famous for silk.

Statue of Gainsborough in Market Hill

St. Gregory's, the mother church of Sudbury, stands in a quiet area at the west end of town. It was built by Simon of Sudbury on the site of a wooden seventh-century church. Who was Simon of Sudbury? The Archbishop of Canterbury. He was beheaded by the Wat Tyler rebels during the Peasants' Revolt in 1381. His head was displayed on London Bridge for six days and then sent back to Sudbury where it is still displayed in a case in the vestry. In a less grim vein, the church contains a medieval font cover of ingenious design. Highly ornamented, it rises in stages to a height of about twelve feet.

116

The lowest stage can be pushed up in telescopic fashion, allowing the font to be used without disturbing the upper part.

All Saints Church, mostly of the fifteenth century, is on the lower part of Friars Street near Ballingdon Bridge. When the churches of Sudbury were rebuilt in the flourishing fifteenth century, the fourteenth-century chancel of All Saints was allowed to remain, and it remains, consequently, the oldest building in Sudbury.

The town has literary associations, for it is the "Eatanswill" of Dickens' *Pickwick Papers*. The Swan Hotel was known as Buff Inn in that novel, and the Rose and Crown (now a cinema and shops) was the Town Arms. John Bunyan, the Puritan writer and author of *Pilgrim's Progress*, reputedly visited Sudbury, staying at the home of his friends the Burkitts in what is now Burkitt Lane.

And it has American associations, for Sudbury was the home of a key figure in the American Revolution. William Dawes arrived in New England in 1635 and eventually settled in Boston. His house in Sudbury Street remained in the possession of the family for five generations, until it was pulled down by the British in 1775 during their occupation of Boston. It was William Dawes, born in Boston in 1745, who made the famous ride with Paul Revere to "spread the alarm through every Middlesex village and farm. . . ."

Earlier, in 1630, a Puritan lecturer from Sudbury, John Wilson, sailed under John Winthrop of Groton to New England. John Winthrop noted in his diary the death through sickness on that voyage of "Jeff Ruggle of Sudbury and divers others of that town." But John Wilson survived to become a leading director of the colony at Charleston and founder of its church.

Edmund Brown, born in nearby Lavenham, had served in the Sudbury, England, church for fourteen years. He became the first minister of Sudbury, Massachusetts, and was probably responsible for conferring on a New England wilderness settlement the name of Sudbury. That was his gesture in carrying a bit of local heritage to the New Canaan.

East Anglia was a Puritan stronghold and a principal source of emigration. But Sudbury sent more emigrants to New England than any other town in East Anglia. Perhaps that is why Sudburians on both sides of the Atlantic are surrounded by such familiar names as Haverhill, Needham, Ipswich, Boxford, Newton, Acton, and Braintree.

Taunton

Taunton is set in Somerset's fertile Vale of Taunton Deane in the midst of an area of exceptional beauty and venerable history. All around are open fields and hills covered with gorse and heather. There are small villages with ancient churches, and there are manor houses and cottages, mostly of red sandstone. Stately homes and castles, as well as abbey ruins and apple orchards abound. For the impressive past, a hill-fort of 1000 B.C. is in the village of Norton Fitzwarren, and Castle Neroche is a prehistoric hill-fort due south of Taunton. For the active present, there is a happy balance of beauty and industry. For instance, the Taunton Cider Company continues an industry which has long supplied the nectar of the west from the fruited lands.

The Quantock Hills, to the north, is a poet's place. William Wordsworth and his sister Dorothy came in 1797 to live in the Quantocks at Alfoxton House; and Coleridge lived just three miles away, in Nether Stowey, in a cottage that is open to the public. Here he wrote "The Ancient Mariner"; nearby Watchet is the small supposed port from which the eponymous character embarked.

When poets have not lived here, they have been inspired by it. Michael Drayton, the seventeenth-century poet, wrote:

What eare so empty is, that hath not heard the sound
of Taunton's fruitful Deane, not matched by any ground?

The county town of Taunton has dominated western Somerset for centuries. It was founded by the Saxon King Ina. Having defeated the British king of Dumnonia, he built a castle in 710 for the defense of his kingdom. But only twelve years later, his fortress was destroyed.

The town prospered under the protection of the Bishops of Winchester in Norman times, and the massive Taunton Castle was established in 1138.

With all of the comings and goings through this gateway to the west of England, Taunton was never able to turn its back to tumultuous events and was always involved in dramatic happenings. In 1497, an insurgent army of Cornishmen, marching to London, nearly one hundred fifty miles away, to protest taxation, were defeated at Blackheath. In the same year, Taunton was the center of the rebellion when the pretender Perkin Warbeck claimed to be Richard, the second son of Edward IV, one of the little princes murdered in the Tower. On his way to London to seize the crown, Warbeck met his demise at Taunton.

Taunton was involved in the Civil War of the 1640's and changed hands several times. In 1642 it was captured for Parliament, and the following year it was taken for the King. In 1645 began a year-long siege with the Parliamentarian leader, Admiral Robert Blake, hero of the Taunton siege, fighting and defending the town against the king's forces. At the Restoration, Charles II deprived the town of its Charter and dismantled the castle except for the Great Hall and Gateway. (A second Charter was granted in 1677.)

The Monmouth Rebellion followed forty years later. James, Duke of Monmouth, was proclaimed king of England in Taunton. His invasion was defeated at the Battle of Sedgemoor in 1685. But the retribution was severe. Judge Jeffreys tried 509 supporters of the Monmouth Rebellion, and, in the Bloody Assizes of 1685, hundreds were condemned to death. Hundreds more were deported to the West Indies for life. The trials took place in the castle, which is still the center of Taunton.

From the wide, busy shopping street, the narrow Castle Bow passes under a portcullis to the Castle Green. This archway was the main entrance to the castle in medieval times. In modern times, new is imposed on old. The Castle Green, no longer green, is a parking area. In the midst of all that antiquity, a modern sign informs: "Ladies Toilet in Castle Walk 130 yards to the right."

Castle Bow

119

The market, formerly held in the Castle Green, has been moved to another part of the town where the sale of thousands of sheep, pigs, and livestock as well as produce and general goods continues to take place on Saturdays. So Taunton has remained an important market center for over a thousand years.

The castle itself is now the Somerset Museum. The main exhibition hall is the Great Hall where the voice of Lord Chief Justice Jeffreys once bellowed out his sentences and where, according to legend, his ghost still walks on nights in September, the month of the Bloody Assize. The Museum houses relics of local history, a variety of collections including ancient pottery, musical instruments, costumes, Stone and Bronze Age antiquities, and a portrait of King Charles I and his queen by Van Dyke.

On another side of the Castle Green is the Castle Hotel. With walls that date back to about 1300, it offers architectural interest as well as culinary appeal and comfortable elegance. Nearby, the Norman Garden contains part of the walls of the inner moat of 1160 and a square Norman well. Just beyond is the River Tone, which runs down from the Brendon Hills in the west to flow through the center of Taunton and give the town its name.

While the castle is the center of Taunton, there are many other points of interest throughout the town. Two church towers dominate the skyline.

The imposing parish church of St. Mary Magdalene was built toward the end of the fifteenth century when Taunton had developed a thriving wool trade. Its magnificent red sandstone tower is enhanced by the approach from the eighteenth-century Hammet Street, a street of perfect Georgian elegance. The great west tower, 163 feet high, was built in 1503. To prevent possible collapse, it was rebuilt in 1862 in exact replica. The interior of the church features the fan-vaulted ceiling of the tower and a beautifully carved black oak roof. Fifteenth-century glass glitters from the great clerestory windows.

The Church of St. James is also handsome. Probably in existence in 1127, it has been so altered and rebuilt that little remains of the ancient structure. The present building dates from the fourteenth and early fifteenth centuries. Its tower too, the outstanding feature of the exterior, was rebuilt and reproduced in 1873. Inside, ancient timbers support a barrel roof, an unusual feature in Somerset churches. A fifteenth-century font is carved with figures relating to the Christian story, and a Jacobean pulpit is carved with non-Christian mermaids.

There are two sets of almshouses. In Magdalene Street, are Huish's Almshouses, founded in 1615 by Richard Huish, a London merchant. Gray's Almshouses were founded in 1635 by Robert Gray of London, who was born at Taunton.

Also of interest in the town center is the Tudor House, an impressive example of medieval domestic architecture with gables and half-timbered construction, and with parts of it dating to the fourteenth century. If it is true that Judge Jeffreys dined here during his Bloody Assize, it is appropriate that the oldest house in Taunton is now a restaurant.

To the over-exciting events of the seventeenth century must be added a coda—the offshoot of Taunton in America. In the new world, Cohannet was purchased in 1630 by settlers who thanked God for bringing them "over the great ocean into this wilderness from our dear & native land . . . and in honor and love to our dear and native country," their report continues, "we called this place Taunton."

The American city of Taunton has outgrown the mother town in size, population and industry. But the old, formerly-tumultuous town of Taunton has earned its tranquility.

Toppesfield

A Saxon chieftain named Topa or Toppa is undoubtedly the source for the name of this village, which has been variously called Toppesfend, Toppesford, and Thopefield. It is *not* the topmost village in the county. Located in the northeastern corner of Essex, Toppesfield is in a rather flat agricultural area, about fifty miles from London.

In 1905, the Reverend H. B. Barnes, a former Rector of St. Margaret's Church wrote a description of the village in a "Sketch of Toppesfield Parish, Essex Co., England" in which he decried the fact that the town was struggling in the midst of an agricultural depression. He deplored the neglected state of a village being abandoned by the young who leave it in search of employment elsewhere. The situation seems to be still applicable today.

Off the main road, it is a desolate village which seems to be suffering still from depression, agricultural or otherwise, which entices the young to move elsewhere. Even the pump in the town center seems lonely. And the church is

Town Pump

122

locked when not in use. As you enter the church yard through an attractive lych gate, you see the rather unattractively-faced walls of the church building, enclosed by the surrounding council houses and school. Only the village hall opposite the church seems to be a beehive of activity. And perhaps the conspicuous red telephone booth in the center is another source of activity.

Reverend Barnes described the poor condition of the church:

> The body of the church has nothing to recommend it, the seats are mean looking and uncomfortable to use, the pulpit is commonplace, the west gallery . . . while all built of oak is faced on its pillars with carved oak; the great oak beams which span the nave are similarly cased, and unhappily neither they nor the roof are in a sound condition.

Church of St. Margaret

Nevertheless, the fourteenth-century church of St. Margaret offers an impressive distant view of its brick tower with four corner pinnacles, of 1699. The body of the church was built in the early sixteenth century. Inside are several brasses in the chancel, a thirteenth-century monument of a cross-legged knight in armor, fifteenth-century stained glass, and the well-preserved parish registers which date back to 1558.

123

The names of Samuel Symonds and his wife Dorothy can be found in the register as well as the baptism records of their ten children, born between 1621 and 1633. Samuel Symonds later retired to New England, where he was granted a farm of five hundred acres, partly within the bounds of what later became Topsfield. It was he who brought about the change of name to the area settled in 1639 as an offshoot of Agawam, early name of Ipswich. In 1650 the site received its new name—Topsfield—for Symonds remembered with gratification his former home, even if he did not remember its spelling.

"What is its future to be?" the Reverend Barnes asked of Toppesfield and proceeded to make this prediction:

> Automobilism, or electric railways, will make travelling easy, and then this corner of Essex, with its healthy climate, its quiet beauty, its fertile soil, its fine oaks and other trees will attract the class of persons who want a nice house and a few acres of land. Then land will again fetch in this district ten times what it fetches now; then there will be plenty of employment in stables, gardens and pleasure farms for the men who now flock into towns. But this will not be in my day.

Nor has his prediction of an influx of wealth come to pass in our day. Nevertheless, the fulfillment of the prediction is beginning to be apparent; old houses are being renovated, new ones are being constructed. The forecast may be a trifle premature, the changeover slow; but the growth and development of an area rich with resources and qualities is inevitable. A sense of the past is leading to ascent of the future. Already, Reverend Barnes' *Sketch* is, happily, in need of updating and revision.

Truro

The one-hundred-year-old city of Truro is nearly one thousand years old. While the *town* of Truro received a Charter from Henry II in 1156, it was declared a *city* only as recently as 1877. In fact, its cathedral dates from 1880. The contrast of old and new is characteristic of Truro today.

For the flavor of the distant past, there are crooked streets in the area between the cathedral and the river. Another kind of flavor can be had in a small bakery in the shadow of the cathedral which makes two distinctively Cornish biscuits known as Cornish gingerbreads and fairings.

The cathedral, with its three spires, rises above the encroaching, narrow streets and slate-roofed houses and dominates this capital city of Cornwall. Completed in 1910, it was the first cathedral to have been built in England since London's St. Paul. When the decision was made to restore to Cornwall a diocese of its own, a diocese which was lost over eight hundred years ago when it was merged with Exeter, Truro was chosen for its central position in the county.

Not the style of the cathedral, but its materials are Cornish—granite primarily. Though only a century old, it is indeed reminiscent of great medieval cathedrals of France. In design and in spirit, the cathedral links the present to the past. The line of the nave bends at a slight angle to the chancel to accommodate the existing street.

Built on the site of the sixteenth-century parish church of St. Mary, it incorporates most of that ancient south aisle into the new building, giving it a warmth and character that is normally lacking in a totally new and sterile construction. St. Mary's aisle still has a little ancient stained glass, a seventeenth-century alms box, Communion table, and monumental brass. Other old bits include an eighteenth-century organ and pulpit. Brasses and monuments date from 1567 and parish registers, from 1597. In the Jesus Chapel of the cathedral is an altar painting of Christ blessing Cornish industry. It is a new treatment of an old subject which appears on many walls of old churches in Cornwall.

The town's wealth emanates from its location as the center of a rich tin-mining district. Truro was a medieval "coinage" town. By order of King John, tons of tin ore would be brought here from the mines to be tested and stamped. A corner (French, *coin*) of each block of tin was cut off for testing by officers who would certify that the quality met the set standards. By the end of the sixteenth century, the assaying and "coining" of a third of the Cornwall tin was done in Truro. Its prosperity is shown by the Charter

Truro Cathedral

granted by Elizabeth in 1587 for two weekly markets and three fairs.

The shipping of tin and copper ore from Truro was another source of wealth. But the town suffered a serious decline when it lost its trade to the rival port of Falmouth in the seventeenth century. Like Falmouth, Truro is located on the River Fal, but further inland, away from the hazards—and the conveniences—of the sea.

The fortunes of Truro revived in the eighteenth and nineteenth centuries, and the town's present beauty and charm derive from the prosperity of this period. Wealthy merchants built their magnificent Georgian mansions, and a few gave their names to its streets—the Boscawens and Lemons. The town's Georgian past is still to be seen in the gracious Lemon Street, in the cobbled Boscawen Street, and in High Cross.

126

The name of Truro itself has had many variations in both spelling and meaning. Orthographic variations include Triverv, Triueru, Truueru, Treruru, Truru, Trurow, and Truroe. As for etymology, some believe that its name suggests that originally Truro was made up of three streets. "Tri" is Cornish for "three"; and in the first centuries of its existence, from about 1160 to 1460, the town could well have been described accurately as having three streets. Perhaps it meant the "town or castle on the river." In any case, the origin of the name has disappeared together with its Norman castle.

Truro is a commercial center, unrivalled west of Plymouth. In the last century, its mining and mercantile business and the wealth of its gentry gave the town the name of Little London. The compliment is repaid for there is a lot of Cornwall in London, too, where many of the bridges crossing the Thames are made of Cornish granite.

Truro is also the cultural center of Cornwall with an Art Gallery that has paintings by Rubens, Hogarth, Gainsborough and Constable. Yet, for a city, Truro is comparatively small; its population is just over twelve thousand. A brief walk from the city center will take one into the Cornish countryside. It is in a wide valley with villages that are quaint and picturesque in both appearance and name. For example, just over two miles south of Truro is Come-to-Good, named from *cum ty coit,* or the valley by the cottage in the wood. It offers contrast to city bigness and bustle in the whitewashed, simple, open-timbered roof of its Quaker Meeting House built in 1710.

A city of contrasts, Truro may also be contrasted with the American Truro. Not the Cape Cod seaside holiday atmosphere, but a commercial, inland, bustling city center characterizes this capital city of Cornwall.

127

Waltham Abbey

Waltham must be a good name for a town for there are duplications and variations of it on both sides of the Atlantic. In England, there are Walthams in several counties, including Great Waltham and Little Waltham, Waltham-on-the-Wolds and Waltham Cross (which takes its name from the cross erected by Edward I, one of twelve such crosses, in memory of his beloved Queen Eleanor). In New England, there is a Waltham in Maine and one in Vermont. But the Waltham in Massachusetts, on the Charles River, incorporated in 1738, is the counterpart of the ancient town of Waltham Abbey in Essex, on the River Lea.

Waltham Holy Cross was the less popular official name for the pleasant town of Waltham Abbey in England. Located sixteen miles from London, this busy market town was founded by Tovy, standard bearer of King Canute, who brought the "Holy Cross" to this weald-ham or forest homestead.

Tovy made an important abbey town of the existing Saxon settlement of huts built in the clearing by the river. He built a church in about 1040 to accommodate the relic and some three dozen people. But growth was inevitable because of the arrival of pilgrims from all over to the site of the true cross. So while the origins of this ancient town may be rooted in a legend of a miracle, it might have ended life as a legend had not the cross brought about the miraculous growth of a great abbey town.

Tovy's church was rebuilt in about 1060 by King Harold who is said to have prayed here before the Battle of Hastings, perhaps not well enough, for his body was brought here for burial after the battle against the invading Normans. In the Waltham Abbey churchyard is a stone which marks the position where King Harold is believed to be buried. After their conquest, the Normans could not realistically be expected to give the full allotment of respect to the dead king, the last Saxon monarch, and facts are therefore difficult to substantiate. Nevertheless, the fact that Waltham Abbey Church is affectionately known as Harold's Church, would seem to be reason enough to bring the name of Waltham to America.

Why not recall Harold's Church, with its inspiring and romanticized associations, in the new homeland? William Brown, Samuel Livermore, Daniel Benjamin, and others petitioned to have their precinct of Watertown become a separate township with the name of Waltham. Perhaps the new homeland resembled that former home on the River Lea. But it now has the excesses of modern city life—population, industry, and traffic. The City of

128

Waltham Abbey Church

Waltham in Massachusetts today stands in direct contrast to the relatively quiet and ancient-in-appearance town of Waltham Abbey.

Although the Dissolution of the Monasteries, following the break of Henry VIII with the Pope, reduced the Abbey Church of the Holy Cross to a third of its former size, it is the oldest Norman church in England and remains the highlight and glory of the town. Henry II altered the abbey considerably in 1177 when he founded an important Augustinian priory. Thus he sought expiation for the murder of Thomas à Becket. Seven years later, the priory became Waltham Abbey. English royalty came here from the time of Harold up to Charles II. The town took on aristocratic associations and was granted charters for fairs and a market. It grew.

The nine-hundred-year-old abbey is a magnificent ruin. The monastic part, with central tower and transepts, was destroyed in the Reformation, but the nave, having been used as a parish church, is preserved. The solid Norman interior has massive stone piers, some carved with chevron and spiral decoration, to support the arcading and upper clerestory. The east end of the nave has fine stained-glass windows of 1861 by Burne-Jones above the altar and a restored ceiling with signs of the zodiac. The Lady Chapel on the south side of the nave, dating to 1316, survives too with restored fourteenth-century wall painting of the Last Judgment. Remnants of herringbone work on its outside wall are believed to belong to the early church founded by Tovy and incorporated into Harold's Church some twenty years later.

Also surviving are the Abbey Gatehouse and bridge in a picturesque part of the town. The Abbey Gatehouse of 1370, with its wide and narrow entrances for carriages and pedestrians, is a fragment of the ancient monastery.

The Market Place of Waltham Abbey is close to the church. Here the weekly market, first granted by Henry III in the thirteenth-century, is still held, on Tuesdays, in the open space. Also in the Market Square is the fifteenth-century "Welsh Harp." The oak-framed inn dates back to those early times when pilgrims traveling in large numbers to the shrine of King Harold needed accommodation. With lych gate into the courtyard, the inn is believed to have been the guest house of the monastery.

Waltham Abbey was formerly a forest town exclusively for the pleasure of kings. No building was permitted within the Royal Forest of Waltham, and cruel penalties were inflicted on anyone who in any way interfered with forest laws and royal pleasures. Safer to kill a man than a deer. So the town had the favorable position of being an accessible forest town for sovereigns who resided in London, at the Tower, from William of Normandy to Elizabeth I. Henry VIII is said to have been particularly fond of it. Legend has it that he went to the hunt there on the morning of Queen Anne Boleyn's execution.

Gradually, the forest ceased to be a playground for princes, and the town was to develop merely as a market town, a center for Lea Valley produce and cattle. The forest was abused, and it was threatened with being built in or enclosed. It was cut down and its timber used to build ships. But in true English tradition, it was rescued from possible demise. Now called Epping Forest, no shooting is permitted in what was once a hunting forest.

Although it is still the home of deer and other wild life, it is primarily the happily-hunted ground for tame picnickers escaping from London, whose property it became. The Corporation of the City of London acquired Epping Forest, and Queen Victoria dedicated it to the public in 1871.

Waltham tells an inspiring story, and many have been and continue to be inspired by it. Thomas Tallis, the Elizabethan composer, was organist of the abbey at the time of the Dissolution in 1540. John Foxe, author of the famous *Book of Martyrs* lived here. And Tennyson, who lived in nearby High Beech, composed "The Bells," based on his hearing the sounds of the bells of Waltham Abbey Church. A charming if fictional account relates an inspirational tale of another variety; Queen Elizabeth's Hunting Lodge at Chingford, now a museum, was supposedly the royal hunting house in which James I carved a joint of beef with his sword and dubbed it "Sir Loin."

The town still retains its ancient appearance in the midst of twentieth-century industrial life, and Harold's Church is still the center of it all. Waltham Abbey illustrates the progress from a cluster of huts to modern town in just over nine centuries.

Wareham

Small and quaint old Wareham, with its lovely buildings and picturesque quay by the bridge, is known to tourists who pass through. That's the trouble: visitors merely pass through and miss the valuable and pleasurable points of interest.

Situated between two rivers, The Frome and the Piddle, which flow eastwards into Poole Harbor, Wareham, with its obviously defendable setting, was inhabited over two thousand years ago. The ancient Britons settled here, followed by the Romans. But the Saxons made it a place of great importance and fought hard to defend it from the invading Danes. Conflicts with the Danes from about 800 onwards destroyed much of Wareham including its castle and nunnery. After King Alfred liberated it from the Danes who took over in 866, Wareham continued to develop and became an important town with two mints and a wealthy port. Now the harbor is silted up and Wareham lies a mile inland.

The extremely ancient town walls still enclose Wareham on the north, east, and west; the south side of the town was protected by the River Frome. The walls were originally ancient British earthworks. Then the Romans reinforced them with stones, and they remained valuable strategic defenses. Today the earthen walls which surround the town offer fine views of Wareham and glimpses into the past. In the northwest corner, a curved section is believed to have been a Roman amphitheatre. The highest section of the wall is known as Bloody Bank because some of the Monmouth rebels sentenced by Judge Jeffreys were executed on that spot in 1685.

Three old churches remain in Wareham, but Holy Trinity, with its sixteenth-century west tower and fourteenth-century nave, is now disused, and the building has become an arts center.

Lady St. Mary is the church of the Benedictine nunnery founded by St. Aldhelm in about the year 700 and later destroyed. The present priory, located on the south side of the church on the site of the ancient nunnery, is now privately owned. The Church of Lady St. Mary was spoiled by the excesses of the Victorians when they rebuilt it in about 1842. But it contains numerous objects of interest.

In the north aisle is the stone coffin of Edward the Martyr. King of Wessex and England, Edward was murdered in nearby Corfe Castle. His body was buried in Wareham in 978 but later removed to Shaftesbury. Also kept in the church are short stone pillars believed to be remains of pagan altars and a cresset stone of the Middle Ages with little hollowed-out cups

132

which held oil used for burning floating wicks. The parish church of Lady St. Mary has a unique nine-hundred-year-old, six-sided lead font and two thirteenth-century Purbeck marble effigies of knights in armor, cross legged, both of the thirteenth century.

A more modern effigy is in the Church of St. Martin—the effigy of Lawrence of Arabia (T. E. Shaw), who was killed in a motorcycle accident in 1935. Sculptured by Eric Kennington, the recumbent figure is represented in Arab costume, with curved dagger in hand, and head resting on a camel saddle. Lawrence's grave is in the cemetery of Moreton village, and his cottage, Clouds Hill, is seven miles to the northwest of Wareham in Turners Puddle, a name as flamboyant as the person himself.

St. Martin's Church

St. Martin's Church, high on the northern walls, is a Saxon church founded by St. Aldhelm in about 700. Although Saxon parts still remain, the chancel arch and north aisle are of the very early Norman period, and most of the building dates from the twelfth and thirteenth centuries. Medieval

133

paintings cover walls of this, the most interesting of the churches in Wareham.

The town center was largely destroyed in 1762 in a burning reminiscent of London's Great Fire of 1666. Much of the present town is in the simple brick style of the rebuilding, as exemplified in the Red Lion Hotel.

Wareham is arranged in grid street pattern, probably of Late Saxon origin, and the central crossroads cut Wareham into four quarters. The Red Lion is in the western arm or West Street. In the eastern arm, East Street, is located an interesting set of almshouses of 1741. North Street leads up to St. Martin's at the northern entrance of the town, and South Street leads to the river and to Holy Trinity at the southern entrance. In South Street are two of the town's best houses. The Manor House, built of Purbeck stone, of three stories and top balustrade, and set behind railings, is an imposing example of eighteenth-century domestic architecture at its best. Nearly opposite is the Black Bear Hotel, a striking inn of about 1800, with a lovely facade and a columned porch carrying—naturally—a black bear.

Corfe Castle

Wareham is the gateway to the Isle of Purbeck, a puzzle of a name that refers, not to an island, but to the peninsula which extends to the English Channel in the south and west and to Poole Bay in the east. Located 117 miles from London, Wareham and its surroundings contain many literary and historic associations.

Wareham is Anglebury in Thomas Hardy's Wessex. In such works as *The Return of the Native,* the author refers to the stretch of moorlands north towards Dorchester and eastwards almost to Poole as Egdon Heath.

The ruined, romantic Corfe Castle is only four miles from Wareham. It has superb views and a name that means "gap" for it is situated in a break in the Purbeck Hills where the River Corfe and a tributary have isolated the site on which the Castle stands.

A gap of another kind remains which can be happily closed—the gap which exists in the experience of those trippers on their way to holiday places such as Swanage and Bournemouth who rush through the small, sleepy town.

Wareham in Massachusetts was unquestionably named for the Wareham in Dorset, England. The similarity extends beyond the name to the streams of holiday goers who also avoid the newer Wareham as they hurry on to Cape Cod.

Winchester

The massive statue of Alfred the Great, erected in 1901 to mark the thousandth anniversary of his death, dominates the High Street of Winchester; and that is entirely appropriate, for Saxon King Alfred made Winchester the dominant city of England—the capital, in fact. And even when the capital shifted to London, sixty miles to the northeast, by the time of Henry III, kings continued to come, and Winchester continued to be important. Today it is a city resplendent in the riches of history and tradition that make for an unforgettable visit.

Long before King Alfred, the site was an important Belgic settlement in the Itchen valley where the River Itchen goes through a ridge in the chalk hills. Under the Romans, it was given the Latin name of Venta Belgarum—Venta of the Belgae. The Romans, with their strong concern for security, made this tribal center a major town of the area, and Venta became the fifth largest city in Britain. After the beginning of the fifth century, the Saxons occupied the place referred to as Vintanceastir by the Venerable Bede, who traced the ancient history of England to the year 731.

Because the Normans traditionally preserved existing sites of worship, the cathedral overlaps the site of the earlier Saxon church of King Alfred. On low ground, the cathedral is overlooked by St. Catherine's Hill to the south and by St. Giles's Hill to the east, which gives the best panoramic view over the city and the cathedral.

Begun in 1079 and almost continuously rebuilt or remodelled up to the fifteenth century, the cathedral supplies architectural examples ranging from the Early Norman (with the most complete work in the transepts) to the Late Gothic.

Soon after its initial completion in 1200, the eastern part behind the altar had to be enlarged to accommodate pilgrims coming to the Shrine of St. Swithun. The legendary saint is held responsibile, unjustifiably, for England's not-so-legendary rainy weather. The humble Swithun, who died in 802, had requested burial in the churchyard. When monks afterwards tried to remove the body to a more exalted position, a deluge rendered the task impossible, and rain continued for forty days. Amateur meteorologists still maintain that rain on St. Swithun's Day (July 15) will continue for forty days.

The undramatic exterior of the cathedral belies the architectural splendors of the interior. Entering from the west, one is immediately impressed by the massive fourteenth-century pillars from which shafts tower

136

up and soar into the intricate fan vaulting. The resultant feeling of height and grace can be attributed to the remodelling work done under William of Wykeham (1366-1404), who made it the longest cathedral in England, measuring 556 feet in length.

In addition to the spacious and unmatched nave, the priceless treasures of the interior include the original fifteenth-century altar screen, seven exquisitely carved chantry chapels, medieval wall paintings, a twelfth-century black Tournai marble font, the library containing rare and beautiful illuminated manuscripts, and memories of the thirty-five monarchs who dwelt in this ancient capital.

An entire day could be spent profitably inspecting monuments and inscriptions inside the cathedral. Almost as many kings and queens lie buried in this cathedral as in Westminster Abbey. Stone screens in the chancel carry six carved chests that contain the bones of Saxon monarchs. The remains of William II were brought here when he met a violent and mysterious death while hunting in the easily-accessible New Forest. He was buried under the tower with, the records say, "many looking on and few grieving."

In the north aisle is the grave of Jane Austen, and above it on the wall is a memorial tablet and window. Perhaps the most remarkable thing about the inscription is that it makes no mention of Jane Austen the beloved author whose books have brought joy to so many, but refers to Jane Austen the beloved human being: "The benevolence of her heart, the sweetness of her temper, and the extraordinary endowments of her mind obtained the regard of all who knew her and the warmest love of her intimate connections."

In a small chapel of the south transept, the famous angler Izaak Walton lies buried. He is still remembered for his best seller of 1653, to give it the full and fashionably long title, "The Compleat Angler, Or the Contemplative Man's Recreation, Being a Discourse on Fish and Fishing, Not Unworth the Perusal of Most Anglers."

One somewhat amusing epitaph is outside near the path leading to the west front of the cathedral. The inscription on the gravestone of Thomas Thetcher, who died in 1761 "by drinking Small Beer when hot," admonishes:

> Soldiers be wise from his untimely fall.
> And when ye're hot, drink strong or none at all.

Also outside, in the secluded cathedral close, a harmonious blending of various buildings includes a thirteenth-century deanery, a half-timbered Tudor building called Cheyne Court, and the Pilgrim's Hall which was a lodging place in the Middle Ages for pilgrims on their way to Canterbury.

High Street with King Alfred's Statue

Beside the cathedral close is one of the city's two remaining gates, the fourteenth-century Kingsgate with the tiny Church of St. Swithun above it. Clearly, Anthony Trollope had this building in mind when he described the Church of St. Cuthbert at Barchester:

> It is a singular little Gothic building, perched over a gateway, through which the Close is entered, and is approached by a flight of stone steps which lead down under the archway of the gate. It is no bigger than an ordinary room . . . but still it is a perfect church.

Kingsgate leads to College Street, one of the prettiest streets in Winchester. Number 8, a stucco-fronted building looking towards the cathedral, is the house in which Jane Austen died. Also in College Street is the school founded by Bishop William of Wykeham in 1382 to equip boys for entry into New College, Oxford, which he had already established. Winchester College, the oldest public school in the country, is nearly opposite the palace of the bishops of Winchester, Wolvesey, and within the palace grounds stand the ruins of the twelfth-century Wolvesey Castle built by Henry de Blois.

Of the former Norman castle (which was the royal residence), only Castle Hall survives. Inside, a circular board seventeen feet in diameter ostensibly attests to the veracity of the Arthurian legends. Like the legends, King Arthur's Round Table makes a good story, but the facts are highly debatable.

Castle Hall stands near Westgate, the other of the two remaining gates and a grand monument to the times when Winchester was a walled city. From the top of Westgate, the room which houses a small museum gives access to an excellent view of Winchester's High Street, selected by many as *the* street in England with the greatest number of historical associations. Between Westgate at the top of the High Street and the bronze statue of King Arthur at the other end, are a great many features worth exploring: streets with descriptive names include Staple Gardens (formerly "the staple" where wool was marketed) and Jewry Street (the former Jewish quarter). The Royal Oak Inn of 1630 has a subterranean bar and a long, well-worn table that has been in use for several hundred years. From the turret of the old guildhall (now Lloyds Bank), the curfew bell still rings each evening at eight as it has done since the time of William the Conqueror. Godbegot House, with a name of doubtful origin, is an attractive timber-framed Tudor building.

A focal point of the High Street is the early fifteenth-century Butter Cross, the place for the sale of butter and eggs in the past and for Sunday newspapers now. Several lovely old houses are very near the Cross, and just beyond is a covered shopping way or colonnade called the Pentice.

Where the High Street broadens out into the Broadway, beyond the current Victorian guildhall and St. John's Hospital, is the huge and impressive statue of Alfred the Great; he stands in splendid dignity, some eighteen feet high, dressed in Saxon helmet and mantle.

The High Street ends with a stone bridge over the River Itchen, beside which is a watermill built in 1774, now a youth hostel. Further along, at the foot of St. Giles's Hill is the early sixteenth-century Chesil Rectory.

Any tour of Winchester should include what is possibly the finest set of medieval almshouses in the country—the Hospital of St. Cross. Just over a mile from the city center is the foundation established in 1137 by Henry de Blois, Bishop of Winchester and grandson of William the Conqueror. It still provides homes for thirteen poor men, who can be identified by traditional garb: loose gowns, flat hats, and silver crosses. Still another tradition

Godbegot House

provides for the distribution of the Wayfarer's Dole of bread and ale to travelers who apply for it at the Porter's Lodge. Perhaps no longer home-baked or home-brewed, perhaps only a symbolic portion, the tradition nevertheless offers clear evidence of a need for sentiment and stability in this city of memories—the same need which prompted emigrants to choose old and familiar English names for their new homes in America.

Woburn

Old Woburn, which dates from Saxon times, was the site for the founding of a great Cistercian abbey in 1145. The village grew steadily up to Tudor times, then declined. But with the coming of the stage coach, *the* method of travel in the eighteenth century, it revived as a coaching town and was largely rebuilt in distinctively handsome Georgian style. The coming of the railways brought an end to coaching and to the revitalization of Woburn. As seen today, it remains the elegant Georgian village it once was.

An attractive High Street preserves many fine buildings. The Bedford Arms Hotel is a dignified eighteenth-century coaching inn, a main staging post on the road from London to the North. It was rebuilt after a fire of 1724 destroyed most of the town. But the signpost of the inviting Bolyn Tea Rooms boasts of its "XVI Century" origins. For another kind of drink, pubs are plentiful. So are attractive shops. The bay-fronted butcher's shop, formerly the Goat Inn, is particularly pleasing. Tudor buildings with eighteenth-century facades house antiques and boutiques and encourage the tourist trade. And nearby Woburn Abbey, with thousands upon thousands of visitors each year, has insured the twentieth-century revival of the town of Woburn.

Woburn Abbey was given to the Russell family, Dukes of Bedford, by Henry VIII after the monastery was dissolved. But not until the seventeenth century did the Russells come to Woburn to live. In 1626, when the plague was raging in London, the family fled to their home in the country to escape infection. They liked it and decided to rebuild the abbey as a family residence. Remodelled and reconstructed several times since then, the present house, built around a quadrangle on the monastic site, dates from 1746.

The stately home stands in the middle of a park of some three thousand acres in which eleven varieties of deer roam freely. The house was passed through succeeding generations to the present Duke of Bedford, who inherited the abbey along with £5,500,000 worth of death duties. Crippling taxation forced him to open the house to the public in 1953, and now visitors may feast on the priceless collections of art treasures contained within.

Paintings include works by Van Dyck, Rembrandt, Reynolds, Gainsborough, Velazquez, and Holbein. The dining room in the Private Apartments is called the Caneletto Room because it contains twenty-one

Woburn High Street

142

views of Venice commissioned when the painter Caneletto came to England in 1746.

State Apartments have gilded ceilings, French and English eighteenth-century furniture, and a vast variety of art treasures. Queen Victoria's State Bedroom, as it became known after Queen Victoria visited with Prince Albert in 1841, is richly furnished.

The China Room displays dark blue and gilt Sèvres dinner service, the most complete set of this quality in existence anywhere. It was presented by Louis XV in 1763 when the Duke was the English Ambassador at the signing of the Treaty of Paris.

A curious grotto exemplifies shell rooms which were so popular in the seventeenth century. Thousands of shells set in stucco are arranged in patterns to decorate walls and ceilings of a room which was originally open to the garden.

The present Duke is not without a touch of showmanship. The estimated cost of £1000 a day for the upkeep of Woburn Abbey is met by the entrance fees of the throngs who arrive for a pleasurable day's outing. With ducal dignity, he has created a Wild Animal Kingdom which allows visitors to drive through the safari park among lions and tigers. He has also installed a crafts center, an antiques center with about fifty shops, a passenger train, and restaurants—all designed to obtain revenue needed to preserve the sumptuous setting for posterity.

Not in the Wild Animal Kingdom of Woburn in England, but in the wilderness of seventeenth-century New England, was there a need to preserve the name of the place in Bedfordshire which produced emigrants to Massachusetts. Captain Edward Johnson wanted to honor his friend, Major-General Robert Sedgwick, who came from Woburn in 1635. The General Court met in Boston in 1642 and ordered that "Charlestowne Village is called Wooborne."

Woburn Abbey

144

Worcester

Ask an older, loyal Worcester native about his city and he is almost certain to recall, not without anger or bitterness, some wonderful house or other which was pulled down "for no other reason than that it was standing." So spoke the curator of the Edward Elgar Birthplace Museum. To an outsider, any city that can boast of Elgar and music has enough. But Worcester, despite the mutilation wreaked by so-called city planners, has much more.

Worcester today is a city known for its music and its cathedral, as well as for its china and sauce. It is a modern city with traffic, factories, offices, architectural insults and noise—all conspiring to conceal ancient buildings and rich history.

Worcester must have been much gentler, much quieter, very long ago when it was merely an important ford on the River Severn in pre-Roman times. Its importance rose in Saxon times. The establishment of a Bishopric in Worcester in the year 680 marks the first major historical event. Under the Saxons, when it was known as Wigorna ceastre, the town grew. The Normans were wise enough to retain the Saxon Bishop Wulfstan after their Conquest, and Worcester continued to grow under his leadership and inspiration. Bishop Wulfstan rebuilt the Cathedral in 1084. The crypt of that cathedral remains unaltered—one of the finest examples of Norman work in the country—with its dramatic use of columns and bays.

The chief glory—some would say the only glory—of Worcester is its cathedral. From any distant point of view the cathedral is imposing. It stands on a high bank above a bend in the River Severn, displaying its majestic and massive central tower.

From close up, the site and surroundings are equally impressive. Ancient out-buildings which formerly belonged to the cathedral extend to the river. On the south side of the cathedral, a Norman gateway leads into the cloisters. Beyond the cloisters and the adjoining decagonal Chapter House (c.1140) is College Green, which can also be entered from the street by the gateway of Edgar Tower. It is a quiet refuge where one can quickly forget the noisy streets and view the monastic buildings and ruins. Houses in the Green include the Old Palace in Deansway, ruins of Guesten Hall of the monastery, and the refectory. The refectory of the old monastery has been used by the King's School, founded by Henry VIII in 1541 after the monastery was suppressed. The boys of the King's School provide the voices of the cathedral choir. Across the Severn, on the west bank, is the County

The Cathedral Crypt

Cricket Ground, which affords one of the spectacular views of the cathedral.

Inside the cathedral, a happy blending of design and styles are to be found. The nave was constructed over a period of two centuries—from mid-twelfth to 1377. The two westernmost bays of the nave date to about 1160 or 1170. An unbroken view of the high vaulted roof with pointed arches on pillars stretches for a distance of over four hundred feet to give the satisfying feeling of harmony and proportion.

The choir was begun in the thirteenth century. It contains fourteenth-century choir stalls with one of the finest sets of misericords in England, giving carved representations of ordinary life in medieval times.

In the center of the choir is the tomb of King John, who died in 1216. His effigy in Purbeck marble is the earliest royal sculptured figure in England. King John had requested burial in the cathedral of his favorite city.

Another royal memorial is Prince Arthur's Chantry, built by Henry VII in memory of his eldest son. It is an appropriate spot to meditate on what the course of history might have been. After the premature death of Prince

Arthur in 1502 at the age of fourteen of pneumonia, his young widow, Katherine of Aragon, became the first of the wives of Arthur's younger brother, Henry VIII.

Other buildings of great architectural merit and historical interest exist in various parts of the city center.

An impression of the medieval city which prospered as a cloth-weaving center can best be seen in Friar Street. It contains the finest group of early timbered houses now remaining in the city, evidence of the riches derived from sheep.

The Greyfriars, originally the guest house of the friary, was built in about 1480. Saved from demolition by Mr. Matley Moore and his sister, it has been lovingly restored by them and is now maintained by the National Trust. The still spry Miss Moore shows visitors around on specified days of the year.

On the opposite side of the street is the Tudor House Museum, a sixteenth-century timber-framed building with molded plaster ceiling and exposed example of the original wattle-and-daub construction. The Museum displays life in Worcester from Elizabethan times.

Two houses in the city have royal associations. In the continuation of Friar Street, in New Street, is the King Charles House. Through its back door the uncrowned Charles II escaped after his disastrous defeat at the Battle of Worcester, with Cromwell's troops in hot pursuit.

On the corner of Queen Street and the Trinity stands Queen Elizabeth's House, again a half-timbered house. She visited in 1574 and tradition has it that she addressed the crowds from its open gallery.

Worcester seems to have made little provision for pedestrians. If one can safely cross the street to get there, at the end of Friar Street, in Sidbury, is the Commandery. Perhaps the most famous of the city's black-and-white buildings, its Great Hall with oriel windows and minstrels' gallery is impressive. A carved oak Elizabethan staircase leads to an upper room with a sixteenth-century wall painting. Originally the Hospital of St. Wulfstan founded in 1085, its odd name is believed to derive from the title taken by Masters of the Hospital from about the thirteenth century who called themselves Commanders.

The Berkeley Hospital is one of the loveliest groups of almshouses in England. It was founded in 1692 by Robert Berkeley, grandson of Judge Berkeley who left six thousand pounds for that purpose and whose statue stands at the far end of what appears to be a pretty Netherlandish picture by Peter de Hooch.

Another building to admire is the Guildhall in High Street. Rebuilt in

147

1721-24, it has statues of Charles I and Charles II in niches on either side of the entrance, while a carving depicts Cromwell's head nailed by its ears above the doorway; in a niche between two upper center windows is a statue of Queen Anne, garbed in brocaded dress.

The Elgar Birthplace Museum

From Worcester, King Charles managed to escape. From Worcester, the Severn escapes. But Worcester offers musical escape too. Sir Edward Elgar was born in 1857 in Upper Broadheath, just three miles outside the city. His cottage, with its inspiring view of the Malvern Hills, has become the Elgar Birthplace Museum and contains many items associated with the composer who made an immeasurable contribution to English music. His father kept a music shop in Worcester at 10 High Street, now occupied by the department store of Russell and Dorrell.

The tribute to music doesn't stop there. Worcester is known for its Three Choirs Festival which it shares with Hereford and Gloucester. Held in turn each year in each of the three cities, the Festival claims to be the oldest in existence. It traces its origins back to the early eighteenth century when it began as a charity to help orphans and widows of the clergy. It continued to evolve from 1715 as London artists began to supplement the provincial choirs. Significantly, Elgar has remained an inspiration, and his music is well represented in the Festival performances. A window in the cathedral with the theme of "The Dream of Gerontius" commemorates him.

In addition to this cultural feast, Worcester is also world famous for at least two items useful in a material feast. The chemical experiments of Dr. John Wall (who died in 1776) resulted in a formula for the improved manufacture of china which led to the present Worcester Royal Porcelain Company.

Worcestershire Sauce dates from the early nineteenth century from a secret recipe brought back to England by Lord Sandys, a former governor of Bengal. He asked the chemists Lea & Perrins to make up a sauce from that recipe. They consented. But the finished product was found to be so unpalatable that they—because the English never throw anything away—relegated the jars to their cellars. A fortunate accident occurred when they came across those sauce jars some years later and decided to taste it again before discarding the disagreeable stuff. The sauce, having matured, was absolutely superlative!

Another successful commercial venture is the still popular local newspaper, *Berrow's Worcester Journal,* which has been publishing since 1709.

It is perhaps a more idealistic venture which binds the two Worcesters irrevocably. In Massachusetts, on October 15, 1684, the General Court granted that the Indian name, Quinsigamond, be superseded by "Worcester"—a name believed to have been suggested because it was the English birthplace of some of the committee members or settlers. Other sources believe that the Massachusetts city was named after the Battle of Worcester, fought on the Worcester Plains in 1651 between the forces of King Charles II and Cromwell.

The nearby village of Droitwich was the home of Edward Winslow, a Mayflower emigrant who later became Governor of Massachusetts. A memorial to him is in St. Peter's Church in Droitwich.

So while many lament that the jumble of Tudor houses that once distinguished Worcester has been replaced by a modern jumble of commercial developments, multi-story car parks, and tortuous traffic patterns, there is nevertheless a great deal to justify making the 110-mile trip from London—or the trip across the Atlantic.

Wrentham

This small Suffolk village consists essentially of a long main street (the High Street) strung out along a main highway (the A12) which is lined with houses, inns, a town hall, and shops. The road was constructed in the old coaching days toward the end of the eighteenth century when Wrentham was a stage on the turnpike road from London to Ipswich to Yarmouth. The stage coaches may be gone, but the busy road maintains steady streams of traffic, particularly in the summertime, from travelers to the coast.

Just three quarters of a mile away from the business and traffic of the village center, in a peaceful and pretty place, is the Parish Church of St. Nicholas. Its Perpendicular tower can be seen from a distance. Indeed, it was used as a signal tower to give warning of invaders in 1804 when England felt threatened by the Napoleonic invasion. While that scare came to nothing, the only real invasion remains that of holidaymakers rushing through Wrentham on their way to coastal resorts. Drivers in a hurry who do stop at this former coaching village can find recompense.

The Church of St. Nicholas, built on a Saxon site, is first referred to in Norman times. The exact date of building is not known, but it was extended in about 1260 with the addition of a chancel and expanded again in the fifteenth century when Wrentham prospered. At that time, the large Perpendicular tower was built too.

In 1853 the church was again extensively restored and the north aisle added. This newest part contains some of the oldest stained glass in the church, dating from the fifteenth century. One medieval picture of the patron saint of the church shows St. Nicholas, clasping his staff and mitre, with a child seated on his knee. Another bit of ancient glass depicts in exquisite detail an unknown saint.

The church has lovely touches everywhere. The tower doorway must be singled out for its beautiful carvings; and the nave, for its clustered columns. Bearded heads are in the roofs, and two old memorial brasses are in the floor. Ele Bowet of 1400 is engraved in brass dressed in a long robe with bell-shaped sleeves, and Humphrye Brewster is decked out in Elizabethen armor. The Brewster family built Wrentham Hall in 1550 (now demolished) and made this one of the influential English centers of Puritanism.

Reading through the visitors' register in the church, one might come away with the impression that the only travelers to stop speeding and start looking come from Wrentham, Massachusetts. A connection is certain.

John Phillips, Rector of Wrentham in Suffolk went to Salem in 1638 where he stayed for about three years before returning to his former parish where he died in 1660. Indeed, many former residents of Wrentham in Suffolk left for the antipodean retreat from about 1660. In 1673, Wrentham in Massachusetts was created a town. It seems a form of retribution that the pattern has now been reversed: American visitors, full of reverence, return to Wrentham origins.

York

Just over nineteen hundred years ago, a Roman legion established a fortress on the banks of the River Ouse for defense in the north of England. They ousted a powerful British tribe, the Brigantes, who had been settled in the area for centuries. Thus began, in the year 71, Eboracum, the place of the yews—or York.

The city became one of the most important in the Roman Empire. The Roman Emperors Hadrian and Septimus Severus came to Eboracum, and Constantine the Great was here proclaimed Emperor in 306. Of the few visible traces that remain of the Roman city, the most impressive is the Multangular Tower, the west corner of the fortress. So much for the grandeur that was Rome.

After the Roman legions withdrew near the start of the fifth century, several successive waves occupied this important center. It was the Saxon city of Eoforwic when King Edwin, a convert to Christianity, built the first church in 627 on the site of the present cathedral. Danish invaders took over in 876 and made Jorvik (or York) their capital city. Old street names too have persisted from these times. The main shopping thoroughfare of Coney Street was Conynge Strete, a name derived from the same root as the German word *König* or king; it was the king's highway. Goodramgate is named after Guthrun, a Danish chieftain. The Scandinavian suffix *gate*, meaning street, is commonly found in many of York's street names: Petergate, St. Saviourgate, Swinegate. Micklegate means Great Street, and Stonegate may have been so named because it was stone-paved.

Alas, poor Jorvík fell in 944 when Edmund conquered Northumbria and made it part of the Anglo-Saxon kingdom.

Under William the Conqueror, the Normans built two wooden castles atop earth mounds to subdue the rebellious population. The mound which survives on the west bank of the Ouse is known as Baile Hill. The other is Clifford's Tower, a thirteenth-century stone keep. The original Norman castle on that mound was tragically destroyed in 1190 when the Jewish community of York sought sanctuary there. They set fire to the castle and died in the flames rather than be slaughtered by the bloodthirsty mob. A Jewish boycott of the city of York ended as recently as 1978, with a joint ecumenical service in Clifford's Tower.

The medieval core has persisted through the centuries to give a unique and savory flavor to the modern city center. Much of the medieval thirteenth-century stone wall which surrounded the city can still be walked upon, and a number of bars or gates are in good condition. The wall between Bootham Bar and Monk Bar is the most attractive part to walk on. Walmgate Bar is the only one in England with its barbican intact. Invaders passing through the narrow channel made by the outward extension and gateway of the barbican were subjected to a barrage of missiles.

Clifford's Tower

Micklegate Bar was entered by those approaching from the south, and on this gate were displayed severed heads of traitors impaled on spikes. Shakespeare has Queen Margaret exclaim in *Henry VI* of Richard, Duke of York:

> Off with his head, and set it on York gates;
> So York may overlook the town of York.

In fact, heads of executed rebels were exhibited as late as mid-eighteenth century. From an aesthetic point of view, however, Micklegate Bar is appealing enough to allow for suppression of associated horrors.

Within the walls of the city, a tangle of streets, churches, guildhalls, and historic buildings provide a medieval atmosphere. The Shambles is one of the best-preserved medieval streets in Europe. The name is a corruption of Fleshammels (from the Old English word, *shamel*, meaning

The Shambles

slaughterhouse); it was the street of the butchers. Now it is the street of the tourists. Timber-framed houses with jettied stories almost touch across the road, making it possible for persons to lean out from upper stories on opposite sides of the street and shake hands. The Butchers' Hall is at Number 40. Number 35 was the home of the saint of York, Margaret. Alleged to have hidden Jesuit priests, she was martyred in 1586 by being pressed to death under a heavy door on which were piled stones. The house of Margaret Clitherow is now a chapel and a moving shrine to this canonized butcher's wife.

Whip-Ma-Whop-Ma-Gate is York's shortest street with the most photographed name plate. Its curious name may have derived from the whipping of petty criminals on the site.

Stonegate is a particularly fine street. It started life as the Via Praetoria, the great Roman Road from Londinium in the southwest, crossing the river to lead to the headquarters of the legion. Mulberry Hall of 1434 probably belonged to a rich merchant and is indicative of the prosperity of the medieval city. Number 33 was a printer's house, and the so-called Stonegate Devil squats under the eaves. The oldest dwelling house in York, the Twelfth Century House, stands behind Stonegate and is reached through a narrow passage.

Some eighteen churches remain of the fifty which existed in York in medieval times. Another building of medieval note is the Merchant Adventurers' Hall, where wool, England's chief export, was brought to be weighed. No longer powerful overseas traders, the company is today more of a social body. But the Merchant Taylors' and Butchers' guilds are still active.

Also active is the ongoing series of the York Cycle of Mystery Plays, a set of religious plays believed to date from the middle of the fourteenth century. The ruined St. Mary's Abbey, of about 1270, with great empty windows and richly carved arcading, is the effective backdrop for the triennial performance of the York Mystery Plays. And in the grounds of St. Mary's Abbey is the Yorkshire Museum.

In medieval as well as in contemporary times, the city was dominated by its Minster. One of the majestic cathedrals of the world, York Minster sits on top of the remains of the Roman legionary fortress. The church was an outlying missionary run by a group of clergy. It was the mother church of the whole of the North of England ministering to the people—hence its fitting title, *minster*.

The cathedral took over two and a half centuries to build and was completed in 1472. The dimensions (over five hundred feet long, nearly two hundred fifty feet wide across the transepts, and over ninety feet high) make it the largest Gothic church in England.

The stained glass of York Minster is glorious. In the south transept is a circular window commemorating the marriage of the Lancastrian Henry VII and Elizabeth of York in 1486 which ended the Wars of the Roses. The largest thirteenth-century window in the world is in the north transept. Over five feet wide and fifty feet tall, it is called Five Sisters because is it made up of five lancets of grayish-green or grisaille glass with colored geometric patterns. In the nave is a priceless collection of fourteenth-century stained-glass windows, and the great west window (which dates from 1338) is called the Heart of Yorkshire, for the tracery has the form of a heart.

View of York Minster from Goodramgate

The chapter house, of about 1300, a vast octagonal building with a conical roof, is a daring architectural feat; external buttresses support the immensely heavy roof without a central pillar.

The cathedral is an endless source of fascination from the various tombs and monuments, astronomical clock, and fifteenth-century choir screen, to the crypt and Undercroft Museum with remains of the Roman Principia building and earlier cathedrals. Steps to the central tower roof can be climbed for satisfying views of the city from this, the highest point of York.

Each century has left its marks and monuments. Micklegate is essentially a Georgian street with many fine town houses belonging to the eighteenth century. But the city's most ambitious Georgian building is in the busy Coney Street—Mansion House, where lord mayors live during their term of office.

Although York was largely bypassed in the nineteenth century by the Industrial Revolution, it did become a leading railway center under the instigation of one man who has had a street named for him, George Hudson. His house at Number 44 Monkgate is on the tourist itinerary.

And the beginning of this century saw the establishment of the Castle Museum, one of the most intriguing folk museums anywhere. The main building was formerly the Female Prison of 1780; and the former Debtor's Prison of 1705, with two projecting wings and central turret, is also part of the York Castle Museum. The contents include a reconstructed Victorian cobblestone street with its apothecary, haberdashery, and other fascinating shop windows; the Edwardian Half Moon Court complete with shops and pub; craftsmen's workshops; and a cornmill which makes the stoneground flour which is sold by the bag.

The city of York petitioned the government in 1641 and 1648 for the establishment of a university. The granting of that request is the most significant event of the twentieth century. With the Elizabethan mansion of Heslington Hall as its nucleus, the University of York was finally opened in 1963.

Twentieth-century York, with its history still visible, is an accumulation of all the previous ages. And the American city of York, Maine—like so many other American cities—is indeed fortunate to be named for one of the most appealing cities in the world. The Maine name was bestowed in 1623 by Christopher Levett, who was born in York, England, in 1576. As Comden and Green might have sung if they had visited: . . . York, . . . York, it's a hell of a town!

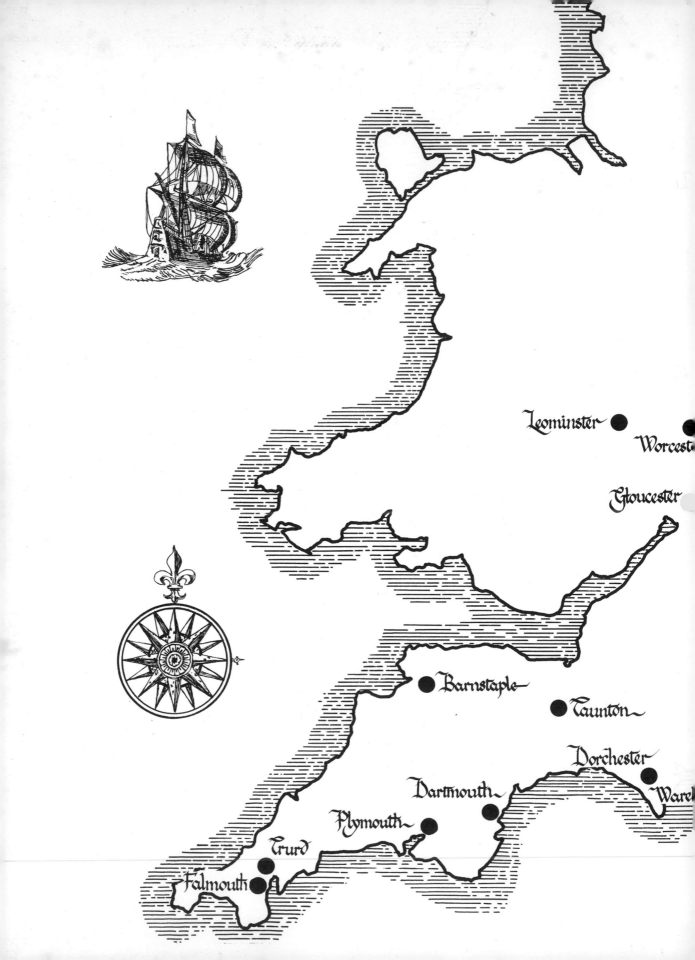

Leominster ●

Worceste[r]

Gloucester ●

Barnstaple ●

Taunton ●

Dorchester ●

Dartmouth ●

Ware[ham]

Plymouth ●

Trurd ●

Falmouth ● A